MORONI'S
GUIDE
TO SURVIVING
TURBULENT TIMES

MORONI'S GUIDE

TO SURVIVING TURBULENT TIMES

JOHN BYTHEWAY

DESERET
BOOK

Interior graphic © Strilets/Shutterstock.com

Visit us at DeseretBook.com

Library of Congress Cataloging-in-Publication Data

Names: Bytheway, John, 1962– author.
Title: Moroni's guide to surviving turbulent times / John Bytheway.
Description: Salt Lake City, Utah : Deseret Book, [2017] | Includes
     bibliographical references.
Identifiers: LCCN 2017040437 | ISBN 9781629722511 (paperbound)
Subjects: LCSH: Mormons—Conduct of life. | Christian life—Mormon
     authors. | Book of Mormon. Moroni—Criticism, interpretation, etc.
     | Moroni (Book of Mormon figure)
Classification: LCC BX8656 .B886 2017 | DDC 248.4/89332—dc23
LC record available at https://lccn.loc.gov/2017040437

Printed in the United States of America
PubLitho, Draper, UT

10   9   8   7   6   5

Contents

CONTENTS

Chapter One

Meet Moroni

One memorable evening, after participating in a fireside in Tremonton, Utah, I strapped myself into my little Hyundai and set out for the drive home. As I proceeded southbound along the Wasatch Front, I marveled at the number of temples I passed along the way.

I thought about each one I might see if I continued down the I-15 corridor, naming them in my mind: Brigham City, Ogden, Bountiful, Salt Lake, Jordan River, Oquirrh Mountain, Draper, Timpanogos, Provo, Payson, and so forth.

When I was a missionary in the early 1980s, part of the standard equipment was a flip chart containing visual aids, quotations, and pictures. One of the illustrations showed all the temples then in existence—there were sixteen, all on one page, and I could name them all from memory. I couldn't possibly name them all today!

On April 6, 1930, the one-hundred-year anniversary of the organization of the Church, Elder B. H. Roberts told the Saints gathered in general conference:

> Seven temples have been erected in various parts of the land of Zion, for a continuance of this holy work, and more will yet be builded. Think what that work may be when there are a hundred temples instead of seven! (In Conference Report, April 1930, 47)

It must have been hard to fathom back then, but here we are, still some years away from the Church's second hundred years, and there are more than 150 temples!

But the thought that wouldn't leave me as I drove that evening was not so much about the buildings. It was about the man, the icon standing atop nearly all of our temples—that solitary figure, the angel Moroni. There he was, all alone, looking out over the valleys like the watchman on a tower that he was. It occurred to me that being alone was something with which Moroni was painfully familiar.

My mind began to race. This may be a family church, I thought, but it was restored through an unmarried teenager who was visited and tutored by an angel—who spent at least the last twenty years of his life as a single adult, alone and wandering for his own safety. Moroni is one of the symbols of our membership. He is on the cover of *For the Strength of Youth, Personal Progress,* and *Duty to God.* How much different would the Book of Mormon be without Moroni's work? I had the thought, *Moroni's best work was done while he was a single adult*—an affirming, comforting, and motivating fact for a large population within our Church. Marital status does not increase or diminish our ability to contribute, and it does not change what the Lord expects of us.

We know that there was limited space on the plates, so what Moroni shared was what was most important to him and what he felt inspired would be important to us. So what was on Moroni's mind as he concluded the Book of Mormon?

I find it fascinating to consider Moroni's unique perspective as I ponder what he wrote to us while in extremely difficult, lonely, and sorrowful circumstances. We might call it Moroni's "last lecture," his final, best advice he had to offer as a voice from the dust.

Not only is Moroni's choice of topics interesting, but the sequence in which they are shared is very instructive, almost like a list of priorities for life. We first hear the voice of Moroni as he begins writing in Mormon 8, and he finishes the book named after his father in Mormon 9. Next, he abridges the book of Ether into fifteen concise chapters. Finally, Moroni concludes the record with ten chapters called the book of Moroni.

This little book will consider Moroni's final contribution, what we might call his "survival guide"—an exploration of Moroni's inspired topics in an inspired sequence, a formula for what we must do to survive and thrive in our turbulent world with all of its challenges. Think about it: ours is a world not unlike Moroni's, full of chaos and violence and seemingly teetering on the brink of destruction. If we can develop a Moroni mind-set, we will navigate those trials more effectively, as he did.

This book is partly a commentary, partly a tribute

to Moroni, and partly an effort to "liken" Moroni's message. For this reason, each chapter will conclude with a section labeled "Likening Moroni," a brief list of ways we might "liken" Moroni's words in that chapter to ourselves (see 1 Nephi 19:23), ways we might apply them as we wander for our own spiritual safety through this latter-day world.

Chapter Two

MORMON 8
"I Am Alone"

Moroni's father, Mormon, was the major abridger of the Book of Mormon, which is why the book appropriately bears his name. One wonders if Moroni had any idea that he would suddenly be called upon to finish his father's work. Given the circumstances, he was in fact the only one who *could* finish the record. The events that overtook him and left his family dead seemed to have come as a surprise. Mormon did not die of natural causes. He was killed in battle at age seventy-three, and so he was not around to finish his book. This is why Mormon chapter 8 begins with these words:

> Behold I, Moroni, do finish the record of my
> father, Mormon. Behold, I have but few things to

write, which things I have been commanded by
my father.

We are left to wonder if this father and son were
together at the moment Mormon died, or when exactly Moroni received these last instructions. We don't
know. Regardless, Moroni knows he must finish the
work his father began.

These first few verses in Mormon 8 contain no
doctrine to speak of, just an outpouring of emotion
and grief. Moroni talks to future generations, using
those yet unborn as a sounding board, it seems, as he
assesses his own situation with this sobering list of facts
(Mormon 8:3–5):

- My father also was killed by them
- I even remain alone
- Whether they will slay me, I know not
- Whither I go it mattereth not
- [I have no] room upon the plates
- Ore I have none
- I am alone
- My father hath been slain in battle, and all
  my kinsfolk
- I have not friends nor whither to go

- How long the Lord will suffer that I may
  live I know not

A pretty bleak picture. With these realities in mind and now engraved upon plates, we know that Moroni is fully aware of his situation. He knows he is totally alone and without resources. He knows he has nowhere to go, and he is unsure about what to do.

Mormon and Moroni had a close and wonderful relationship, as evidenced by the tender words shared in letters preserved for us in Moroni 8–9. It would be difficult enough to experience the death of your father from old age or even an accident, but to have him *killed* in battle, along with "all [your] kinsfolk," is a situation I suspect very, very few will ever experience. But perhaps it was even worse. Was Moroni married? Did he have children? We don't know; it just doesn't say. If he was, then perhaps his wife and children were among those "kinsfolk" also killed in battle. Most of us can only imagine this kind of grief and loneliness. With God as his only friend, somehow Moroni finds the strength to press forward.

A phrase that has come into vogue in the last dozen or so years—a cold but clarifying phrase many of us have used when trying to move beyond our past, assess our present situation, and form a plan for the future—is this:

IT IS WHAT IT IS

Other attitudes we might be tempted to adopt during difficult times might be: "It *shouldn't* be what it is," "It's not *fair* that it is what it is," or "I'm *bitter* about what it is." Each of these attitudes expends valuable energy but leads us nowhere.

Eventually, we are confronted with the fruitlessness of dwelling on the past, and we must straighten our back, fix our gaze, and acknowledge our current circumstances because there is no other alternative—it is what it is.

Having acknowledged all that has transpired, Moroni puts it behind him and looks ahead with these powerful, affirming words:

> Behold, I am Moroni; and were it possible, I would make all things known unto you. Behold, I make an end of speaking concerning this people. I am the son of Mormon, and my father was a descendant of Nephi. And I am the same who

hideth up this record unto the Lord. (Mormon 8:12–14)

These powerful verses indicate a turning point and chart a new course for Moroni. Don't read them too fast! I have probably read these verses dozens of times in my lifetime, but now I see them as a powerful new start for Moroni as he faces a future he likely never imagined. Moroni bravely recognizes the facts and resolutely moves on into that new future. Author Marilynne Todd Linford observed three deliberate steps Moroni takes to plot his new direction:

1. "He consciously stops rehearsing his situation."
2. "He remembers who he is and his heritage."
3. "He defines himself by his work." (*We Are Sisters* [2007], 48)

Yes, "it is what it is." So what do we do with "what is"? There is little use in explaining over and over again to anyone who will listen how bad things are for us. There is little benefit in looping an endless pity playlist of "why me, why this, why now?" Some have taken complaining to an art form. But complaining doesn't do anyone any good unless there is a desire to move on and look to the future. Dr. Laura Schlessinger observed:

> There is effective complaining and ineffective complaining. Ineffective complaining has an intent other than solving the problem. . . . Trying to make things be different by going over them again and again only fixates you in the past. Letting go of that rotting rope with your hand firmly gripping a better philosophy, a wise counselor, or a loving friend or relative as a cheering squad gives you the possibility of greater peace and happiness. (*Stop Whining, Start Living* [2008], 42, 48)

Moroni, by saying "I make an end of speaking concerning this," teaches us that eventually we too must consciously and deliberately "make an end" of that kind of talk. Of course there is a time to mourn, to grieve, to process what has happened—but eventually, that time expires. Then we gird up our loins, fresh courage take, and we "take up our bed and walk." Our questions look forward instead of backward, and we ask, "How do I move on? What can I learn? What do I do? Can I find a way to be useful in these difficult circumstances?" A beautiful lesson in surviving our own times of personal turbulence.

President Howard W. Hunter gave similar counsel when he taught:

> I think it is incumbent upon us to rejoice a little more and despair a little less, to give thanks for what we have and for the magnitude of God's blessings to us, and to talk a little less about what we may not have or what anxiety may accompany difficult times in this or any generation. (*That We Might Have Joy* [1994], 92–93)

Thankfully for his own sake, and for all of us, Moroni finds his voice, discovers his purpose, and speaks powerfully and prophetically to future generations.

I Am the Son of Mormon

As Moroni faces the facts and faces forward, he also finds strength in looking back and remembering his rich spiritual heritage. "My father was a descendant of Nephi," Moroni declares (Mormon 8:13). Which Nephi? The same Nephi who began the record a thousand years earlier, which Moroni will now have the task of finishing. It is commonly believed that

Mormon had such great love for the Moroni spoken of in the war chapters (we often call him "Captain Moroni") that he named his own son Moroni to give him a name and an example to emulate (see Alma 48:17).

We too can find strength in remembering our heritage. One of the great blessings available in the restored gospel is the opportunity to receive a patriarchal blessing, and one of the main purposes of our patriarchal blessing is to declare our lineage and responsibility. Our responsibility is to fulfill the Abrahamic covenant. Elder David A. Bednar taught that going on a mission isn't something we do, it's something we are because we are Abraham's seed (see "Becoming a Missionary," *Ensign*, November 2005, 44–47).

Closer to our day, one of the great benefits of family history is to help us remember the sacrifices of our family members who have brought us to the point where we are now. If Grandma and Grandpa can cross the plains, or if our ancestors can be pioneers in their own way, then perhaps we, like Moroni, can find strength in remembering our heritage when facing a difficult future.

I Know Your Doing

The Moroni who talks to us at the beginning of Mormon chapter 8 sounds a lot different from the Moroni who speaks to us toward the end of the chapter. And, in modern terms, he pulls no punches—he really lets us have it. His voice of mourning becomes a voice of warning:

> Behold, I speak unto you as if ye were present, and yet ye are not. But behold, Jesus Christ hath shown you unto me, and I know your doing. (v. 35)

Moroni has seen the latter days, and what is his reaction? Praise? Admiration? Congratulations? Does he say, "You guys are doing a great job, you're awesome, you're great, you should write musicals about how wonderful you are and pat yourselves on the back"? No. Moroni calls us *all* to repentance.

> And I know that ye do walk in the pride of your hearts; and there are none save a few only who do not lift themselves up in the pride of their hearts, unto the wearing of very fine apparel, unto envying, and strifes, and malice, and persecutions, and all manner of iniquities; and

your churches, yea, even every one, have become polluted because of the pride of your hearts. (v. 36)

Many of my students have asked, "Did Moroni see members of the Church here, or is he condemning the whole world?" When that question comes up, we read the passage again a little more closely. Since the Book of Mormon is addressed to the whole world, as well as to the Church, I think we could assume a little of both. Moroni specifically mentions churches, and those who have "polluted the holy church of God," but also condemns those who are "ashamed to take upon [themselves] the name of Christ" (Mormon 8:38). Perhaps the best answer is, "If the shoe fits, this message is for you." As individuals reading warning words from the scriptures, perhaps we must adopt the "Is it I?" attitude expressed by Jesus' disciples when He announced that one of them would betray Him (Matthew 26:22). We too can ask, "Is it I? Is Moroni talking to me?"

Beware of Pride

Sometimes prophets preach the "pleasing word of God . . . which healeth the wounded soul," and other times, they are burdened to preach the plain word of God which may "enlarge the wounds of those who are already wounded" and condemn us according to our wickedness and abominations (Jacob 2:8–9).

In the general conference of April 1989, President Ezra Taft Benson prepared a classic address called "Beware of Pride." His closing paragraphs included this observation and direction: "Pride is the great stumbling block to Zion. I repeat: Pride *is* the great stumbling block to Zion. We must cleanse the inner vessel by conquering pride" (*Ensign*, May 1989, 7). The importance of conquering pride remains a vital priority for every Latter-day Saint. Some twenty years later, President Dieter F. Uchtdorf endorsed and elaborated on President Benson's words:

> Pride is sinful, as President Benson so memorably taught, because it breeds hatred or hostility and places us in opposition to God and our fellowmen. At its core, pride is a sin of comparison, for though it usually begins with "Look how wonderful I am and what great things I have done," it always seems to end with "Therefore, I am better than you." When our hearts are filled with pride, we commit a grave sin, for we

violate the two great commandments. Instead of worshipping God and loving our neighbor, we reveal the real object of our worship and love— the image we see in the mirror. ("Pride and the Priesthood," *Ensign*, November 2010, 56)

We can almost hear Moroni saying, "Pride destroyed my people, pride destroyed the Jaredites, and pride will destroy you, too." Many of the Lord's choicest blessings are only available to us when we are humble. President Uchtdorf succinctly concluded, "Pride is a switch that turns off priesthood power. Humility is a switch that turns it on" (ibid., 57).

It must have taken a squelching of pride and a tremendous amount of humility for Moroni to accept what had happened to him and his family without becoming bitter and resentful toward God. Certainly Moroni would have preferred to have his father, family, and kinsfolk still around. But Moroni chose to humbly accept his circumstances and seek the will of the Lord in order to know what to do with the remainder of his life, a life that would be lived alone.

LIKENING MORONI
Mormon 8

I will stop rehearsing my past

I will remember my identity

I will find my mission

I will look forward to the future

I will humbly accept the will of the Lord

I will cleanse the inner vessel

Chapter Three

MORMON 9
"Turn Ye unto the Lord"

In Mormon 8, Moroni seems to be saying, "I'm in a bad spot, a difficult place—and it is what it is." In Mormon 9, however, Moroni assures us of his testimony of Christ: "*He is who He is*, and you, future generations, need to know who *He* is." Notice how Moroni wastes no time in directing Mormon chapter 9 to a very specific audience:

> And now, I speak also concerning those who do not believe in Christ. (Mormon 9:1)

The next verse always makes me smile, when Moroni asks, essentially, "Will you believe in Christ when the earth is melting?" (A variation on the "there are no atheists in foxholes" approach—when the crisis is on, watch people get religious!) Moroni becomes a missionary whose teaching pool reaches across the centuries, and his first lesson, to those who may come across this record in the latter days, is their acceptance of Jesus Christ.

I Don't Know What You're Offering, But I Don't Need It

One of the phrases that I heard on my mission, and that I suspect other missionaries have also heard, is, "Thanks, but we don't need that." As we all know, many people don't believe they need religion or spirituality, so their reaction is understandable. If I were to approach you with a glass of water and a couple of antibiotics, you might say, "Why are you giving me that? I don't need that, I'm not sick." President Ezra Taft Benson addressed the common "I don't need that" reaction with this insightful statement:

> Just as a man does not really desire food until he is hungry, so he does not desire the salvation of Christ until he knows why he needs Christ. No one adequately and properly knows why he needs Christ until he understands and accepts the doctrine of the Fall and its effect upon all mankind. And no other book in the world explains this vital

doctrine nearly as well as the Book of Mormon. (*The Teachings of Ezra Taft Benson* [1988], 28)

Suppose we were to approach someone who does not know anything about God, or about Jesus Christ, or about any religion at all, and we say, "Hey, you need to be saved!" Their response might be, "Saved? What do you mean 'saved'? Saved from what?"

The Book of Mormon gives us a model for explaining the gospel to those who don't know about Christ. Moroni and Book of Mormon missionaries like Ammon and Aaron all used the same approach—they each taught about three major events, which Elder Bruce R. McConkie characterized as the "three pillars of eternity": the Creation, the Fall, and the Atonement. Moroni explained:

[God] *created* Adam, and by Adam came the *fall* of man. And because of the *fall* of man came Jesus Christ . . . and because of Jesus Christ came the *redemption* of man. (Mormon 9:12; emphasis added; see also Alma 18:36–39; 22:13)

Why do these pillars matter? Imagine teaching someone that we all need to be saved. They may ask, "Saved from what?" We might respond, "You need to be saved from the Fall." Their next question might be, "You mean autumn? The fall? Did I fall? Fall from what?" We might answer, "Mankind fell from the relationship we had with God in the life before—the relationship Adam and Eve had at the time of the Creation."

THE THREE PILLARS OF ETERNITY:

HOW DID WE GET HERE?
THE CREATION

WHY IS LIFE SO HARD?
THE FALL

WHAT IS THE CURE?
THE ATONEMENT OF CHRIST

We know that Adam and Eve went into the Garden of Eden to fall, and we know that "Adam fell that men might be" (2 Nephi 2:25). The Fall of Adam has been called the "fortunate fall" because of its two directions—downward, but forward. All of this was part of the Father's plan, and without it, we wouldn't be here. Also, the Fall brought with it all kinds of sicknesses and maladies, every genetic disorder of mind and body, and, eventually, death. The Fall includes both physical and spiritual death, and without an adequate understanding of the Fall, we won't adequately understand the Atonement of Jesus Christ.

Moroni seems to be saying, "Bottom line, future reader of these plates, you need Christ. We *all* need Christ. We have been affected by the Fall, separated from God, and we all need the Atonement, or 'at-one-ment,' to allow us to be 'at one' with God again."

Moroni wants future readers to know that not only will Christ atone for our sins, but He will also resurrect and judge. Some may believe God just loves us so much that regardless of how we live, even when we know better, we will eventually be restored to His presence and enjoy happiness. This and similar false doctrines are exposed and discussed elsewhere in the Book of Mormon (see 2 Nephi 28:8–9; Alma 1:4).

I Give Up—I'll Be Sad Now, but at Least I'll Be Happy in the Next Life

The entire chapter of Alma 41 has been called the "Law of Restoration" because it offers a specialized definition of the word *restoration* (a close synonym to *resurrection*). In the context of our mortal existence and the life hereafter, *restoration* does not mean taking something broken and corrupt and restoring it to new or pure condition. *Restoration* means something like, "What goes around comes around." Alma had to explain to his son Corianton that he couldn't live wickedly and expect God to "restore" him to happiness in the next life. "Wickedness never was happiness," he explained (Alma 41:10). (The word *restoration* as used in Alma 41 has nothing to do with the "Restoration of the Gospel," which is another subject.)

Interestingly, Moroni repeats the Law of Restoration in Mormon 9:14:

> Then cometh the judgment of the Holy One upon them; and then cometh the time that he that is filthy shall be filthy still; and he that is righteous shall be righteous still; he that is happy shall be happy still; and he that is unhappy shall be unhappy still.

Here we have another tip for surviving tough times: Do your best to be happy now, in whatever circumstance you find yourself, a challenge Moroni must have grappled with while wandering alone for more than two decades.

If we believe that happiness or even moments of

happiness are not possible in this life because our circumstances are just too hard, Moroni tells us that our unhappiness will be restored to unhappiness. As someone once said, "In life, suffering is mandatory—but misery is optional." Joy in the gospel is possible, even in the midst of our problems, because of Christ (see D&C 101:36).

We might also remember that after Lehi died, when Nephi led his people away from the Lamanites and established the land of Nephi, he explained, "We lived after the manner of happiness" (2 Nephi 5:27). Thus, happiness is not a destination but a mode of travel, a manner of living, or a way of life.

It's human nature to attach our future happiness to events, such as, "as soon as I graduate," or "as soon as I'm married," or "when the kids come," or "when the kids move out." When I was a single adult, I knew many people who thought they would be happier if only they were married, and I suppose I felt that way myself at times. I appreciated this statement from Karen Lynn Davidson: "I have yet to see marriage, by itself, turn an unhappy person into a happy person. A really happy married person is almost always one who was or could have been happy as a single person" (*Thriving on Our Differences* [1990], 39).

In the same way, I suspect we have yet to see college graduation, or a pay raise, or a new car turn someone from an unhappy person into a happy person. Happiness is an inside job.

Don't Do What We Did, 'Cause We're Done

We know from the title page of the Book of Mormon that its major purposes are:

- to *show* . . . what great things the Lord had done for their fathers,
- to *remind* them of . . . the covenants of the Lord, and
- to *convince* the Jew and Gentile that Jesus is the Christ.

But there are also many what we might call "sub-purposes" of the Book of Mormon, and Moroni shares one of them in Mormon 9:31. Moroni, finding himself suddenly inheriting the stewardship of finishing his father's record, feels inadequate, and he expresses it more than once. Moroni knows that he is imperfect, and he is afraid that the message of the gospel may be rejected because of its imperfect messengers:

Condemn me not because of mine imperfection, neither my father, because of his imperfection, neither them who have written before him; but rather give thanks unto God that he hath made manifest unto you our imperfections, that ye may learn to be more wise than we have been. (Mormon 9:31)

Did you catch the wonderful lesson? *Learn to be more wise than we have been!* It has been said that wise men learn from experience, but super-wise men learn from others' experience. The Book of Mormon contains the experience of others, and we can use it and other scriptures to "enlarge our memory" (see Alma 37:8) and become wiser than we would be without them.

LIKENING MORONI
Mormon 9

I will believe in Christ

I will live after the manner of happiness

I will learn wisdom from the experience of others

Chapter Four

ETHER 1–15
"Come unto Me, and
Believe in My Gospel"

What has Moroni taught us thus far? In Mormon 8, Moroni says, "I'm in a difficult situation, but I know who I am and I know what I must do." In Mormon 9, he gives his personal witness of Christ. In presenting the book of Ether, Moroni seems to say, "Now, here's a second witness for Christ, and also a testimony of what happens to individuals and nations when they reject Christ."

Over the years, my students and I have pondered the questions, "Why do we need the book of Ether? Why did Moroni want us to have it? Why did the Lord want us to have it?" As a result of our discussions, we have compiled this list (you may have your own insights and additions to make as well):

1. The book of Ether is a second witness of Jesus Christ
2. The book of Ether is a second witness of how nations fall as a result of rejecting Christ. The Jaredites and Nephites were similar in that:
   - Jaredites and Nephites both experienced the "pride cycle"
   - Jaredites were told to "serve God or be swept off"; Nephites were told to "keep the commandments and prosper in the land"
   - Both civilizations were destroyed by secret combinations
   - Both civilizations learned that wicked kings lead to captivity
   - The Lord in His mercy sent prophets to the wicked in both civilizations
   - The Lord also used famines to bring repentance to both civilizations
   - In both civilizations, the land was cursed when people set their hearts on their possessions

- Moroni and Ether both said in the end,
  "it mattereth not" what happens to me
3. The book of Ether is like a mini Book of
   Mormon—same lessons, same ups and
   downs, same warnings from prophets, and,
   unfortunately, the same apostasy and demise

In the midst of the abridgment of the book of Ether, Moroni cannot resist interjecting some of his own commentary, which comprises most of Ether 12. Moroni was inspired by the words the prophet Ether spoke to the Jaredites, and for good reason. Ether's words gave Moroni hope in his own troubled situation. You've heard this verse before, but this time, read it as if you were Moroni, alone and grieving:

> Wherefore, whoso believeth in God might with surety hope for a better world, yea, even a place at the right hand of God, which hope cometh of faith, maketh an anchor to the souls of men. (Ether 12:4)

Moroni could not fix his current world; he could only hope for a better one. He could not hope for the return of his relatives, the Church, or the Nephites as a people. For them, it was everlastingly too late. Moroni had lost everything—except for the most important thing: his faith. Moroni's belief in God gave him hope for a *better* world, and, eventually, for a place at the right hand of God. That hope was his anchor, and it can be our anchor as well.

Weakness into Strength

Once again in the book of Ether, Moroni reveals his tender heart and his feelings of inadequacy in attempting to complete his father's record:

> When we write we behold our weakness, and stumble because of the placing of our words; and I fear lest the Gentiles shall mock at our words. (Ether 12:25)

Because Moroni expressed his feelings of inadequacy to the Lord, we are all blessed to have the Lord's response preserved for our day:

> My grace is sufficient for the meek, that they shall take no advantage of your weakness; and if men come unto me I will show unto them their weakness. I give unto men weakness that they may be humble; and my grace is sufficient for all men that humble themselves before me; for

if they humble themselves before me, and have faith in me, then will I make weak things become strong unto them. (Ether 12:26–27)

This passage is one of the most repeated scriptures in the Church because of its message of hope. But it is often misquoted, because the word *weaknesses* is often used instead of *weakness*. Is there a difference? I believe there is. *Weaknesses* may imply minor little quirks, habits, or tendencies, whereas *weakness* is a more general statement of our fallen state, which only the grace of Christ can transform. Making weak things strong is the Savior's specialty, and the way we receive such individual help is through humility and a willingness to come unto Christ.

It's interesting to see a similar principle of focusing on a weakness and turning it into strength operating in the temporal world. For example, we remember Captain Moroni of the war chapters (Alma 43–62), who sought to fortify the Nephite cities against attack. His strategy involved looking for weak areas and making them strong.

And in their *weakest* fortifications he did place the *greater* number of men. (Alma 48:9)

The results were wonderful.

But behold, to [the Lamanites'] astonishment, the city of Noah, which had hitherto been a weak place, had now, by the means of Moroni, become strong. (Alma 49:14)

Speaking of making weak things strong, as a bishop, I used to ask the young people I interviewed an interesting question with a military implication: "What's on the threat board?" I learned from a war movie that aircraft carriers maintain something on the bridge called a "threat board" to identify and monitor any possible dangers or enemies within striking distance. In our personal lives, we can ponder where we are weak and ask the Lord to strengthen us in those areas. We should each monitor our own personal "threat board." Is the Word of Wisdom a threat? How about the internet? Am I tempted regarding the law of chastity? Do I tend to gossip? Judge? Resent? Envy?

Identifying the areas where we are weak is one thing—knowing what to do about them is another. Do what Moroni did! The divine formula for conquering our weakness is to take it to the Lord. Do not try to fight your problems and conquer them alone. Do not feel so embarrassed about your sins or your "weakness" that you are unwilling to go to the Lord or His servants for help. Do not neglect the very best source of help because you may feel ashamed. Hiding is not a strategy for healing or growth. Sister Carole M. Stephens taught that "hope and healing are not found in the dark abyss of secrecy but in the light and love of our Savior, Jesus Christ" ("The Master Healer," *Ensign*, November 2016, 10). Express these areas of weakness to the Lord and humbly ask Him for the strength He has promised He will provide.

It's easy to say we believe in Christ, but do we believe Him? Stephen Robinson wrote a classic book a few years ago called *Believing Christ* that challenges us with this very question. We believe *in* Christ, but do we really believe Christ when He promises He can turn weakness into strength? Do we believe Him when He says this wonderful five-word phrase, "I, the Lord, forgive sins" (D&C 64:7)? Among my most thrilling experiences as a bishop were those moments when I felt the Lord's mercy as members came to me to confess a sin or problem in their lives. Elder Neil L. Andersen shared this experience:

> Years ago, I was asked to meet with a man who, long before our visit, had had a period of riotous living. As a result of his bad choices, he

lost his membership in the Church. He had long since returned to the Church and was faithfully keeping the commandments, but his previous actions haunted him. Meeting with him, I felt his shame and his deep remorse at having set his covenants aside. Following our interview, I placed my hands upon his head to give him a priesthood blessing. Before speaking a word, *I felt an overpowering sense of the Savior's love and forgiveness for him.* Following the blessing, we embraced and the man wept openly. I am amazed at the Savior's encircling arms of mercy and love for the repentant, no matter how selfish the forsaken sin. *I testify that the Savior is able and eager to forgive our sins.* Except for the sins of those few who choose perdition after having known a fulness, there is no sin that cannot be forgiven. What a marvelous privilege for each of us to turn away from our sins and to come unto Christ. Divine forgiveness is one of the sweetest fruits of the gospel, removing guilt and pain from our hearts and replacing them with joy and peace of conscience. ("Repent . . . That I May Heal You," *Ensign*, November 2009, 40–41; emphasis added)

When I sat in the bishop's chair, the words that played over and over in my mind were, "Who am I to judge another when I walk imperfectly?" ("Lord, I Would Follow Thee," *Hymns*, no. 220). So I tried as hard as I could to listen as the Savior would listen and to respond as He would have me respond. I was taught about the Lord's willingness to forgive over and over again. Repentance is not something we do *before* we come to Christ; repentance is *why* we come to Christ! We are accepting His invitation. That invitation is to "come as you are, wherever you are." He will take us where we are, but He will never leave us where we are. He will make us better than He found us because He is a healer, both physically and spiritually, with a deep healing that only He can offer. Where else would we go?

Good-bye for the Second Time

At the end of Ether 12, Moroni appears to be giving his final farewell because he closes with these words:

> And now I, Moroni, bid farewell unto the Gentiles, yea, and also unto my brethren whom I love, until we shall meet before the judgment-seat

of Christ, where all men shall know that my garments are not spotted with your blood. (Ether 12:38)

However, after Moroni completes the abridgment of the book of Ether, he continues to bless us with ten additional, wonderful chapters of his own work. How grateful we are that Moroni continued to write! And what does he share in those ten chapters? Oh, nothing much, really, just how to bless, how to baptize, how to organize and run the Church, a couple of letters from his father, a discourse on spiritual gifts, and, of course, Moroni's promise!

LIKENING MORONI
Ether 1–15

I will maintain my faith in Christ

I will not try to conquer my weakness alone—
I will confess my weakness before the Lord,
and He will make weak things strong

Chapter Five

MORONI 1
"I Have Not as Yet Perished"

After abridging the book of Ether, Moroni begins his own book by telling us that he did not expect to be writing anymore, but, he relates, "I have not as yet perished" (Moroni 1:1). So he has decided to continue to give his testimony of Christ and further elements of Christ's gospel to the world.

I Make Not Myself Known

Although alive, Moroni was in danger from the Lamanites. Aware of the threat, Moroni knew he must remain in isolation: "I make not myself known to [my enemies] lest they should destroy me" (v. 1).

This would seem a rather obvious strategy for staying alive—stay away from your enemies. Spiritually speaking, it's a sound strategy as well. Satan puts us not only in mortal danger but in immortal danger, since the consequences of giving in to temptation can be eternal. A thousand years earlier, Moroni's ancestor Nephi expressed a similar thought when he prayed, "Give place no more for the enemy of my soul" (2 Nephi 4:28). Moroni stayed away from his enemies, and so should we. In the Doctrine and Covenants, the Lord said, "Stand ye in holy places, and be not moved" (D&C 87:8). More than just "be in the right place at the right time," this counsel says "be in the right place *all* the time—and *don't move!*"

We don't deliberately venture into Satan's territory. An alcoholic in recovery does not go to bars. A person who cannot swim does not jump into deep water. Moroni's words can be restated by us: *I do not go where my enemies are; I stand in holy places; I don't seek trouble or temptation; I stay away from evil.* However, standing in holy places is more challenging in the latter days. It used to be that we had to go to the great and spacious building to find evil and temptation, but these days, the building comes to us! The building that was floating "in the air" is now "*on* the air," the Wi-Fi, the satellite, the cellular network, and literally in the very air around us. Being surrounded by latter-day telestial media requires constant filtering and constant vigilance.

I Will Not Deny the Christ

Moroni is alive, yet still on the run. "[The Lamanites] put to death every Nephite that will not deny the Christ. And I, Moroni, will not deny the Christ; wherefore, I wander whithersoever I can for the safety of mine own life" (Moroni 1:2–3). Denying Christ is serious business. In the New Testament, Jesus teaches that each of us must eventually take a stand in regard to Christ:

> Whosoever therefore shall confess me before men, him will I confess also before my Father which is in heaven. But whosoever shall deny me before men, him will I also deny before my Father which is in heaven. (Matthew 10:32–33)

Moroni's testimony of Jesus Christ went beyond faith to sure knowledge. He was visited by the Three Nephites, but that's not all. Moroni tells us about another of his visitors whom we will meet at the judgment seat:

And then shall ye know that I have seen Jesus, and that he hath talked with me face to face, and that he told me in plain humility, even as a man telleth another in mine own language, concerning these things. (Ether 12:39)

While few of us have experienced this kind of divine visit, most of us have felt the Savior's enabling power in our lives, and we cannot deny it. Instead, we can be living, breathing visual aids of the fruits of a testimony of Christ. In our conversations with others, both personal and electronic, even in our posts and in our texts, we can be an example of the believers, never letting our allegiance to Christ be censored or too difficult to detect.

When we encounter the world and the worldly, Moroni teaches us to say within our hearts, "I will not deny the Christ. The world seeks to destroy testimonies; I stay away from the world and look for safety."

I Write a Few More Things

What did Moroni do with his time in the waning years of his life? Golf? Cruise? Buy an RV? No, such distractions were not available to him. Moroni's motives were not selfish. He continued to write, to ponder, and to compile the treasures entrusted to him. He dedicated

41

his life to sharing something with people he would never meet in mortality, in hopes that those things would be of worth to "[his] brethren, the Lamanites, in some future day" and to all of us (Moroni 1:4).

My father wrote a ninety-eight-page autobiography, most of it handwritten on yellow pads, which has become a treasure to our family. A few of my children were born after their grandpa passed away, but we are all grateful that he took time to write "a few more things" so that they can come to know who he was and to read about the testimony he treasured.

Author Richard Bach once said, "Here is the test to find whether your mission on earth is finished. If you're alive, it isn't." Moroni had no one to impress by writing a book. But he found a way to bless the future by putting his testimony and experience on the plates.

LIKENING MORONI
Moroni 1

I do not enter enemy territory

I will not deny the Christ

I give something of worth to the future

Chapter Six

MORONI 2
"Ye Shall Give the Holy Ghost"

Moroni's second chapter teaches future generations about the importance of the Holy Ghost to those who desire to follow Christ. He wants us to know that Christ gave His New World disciples power to confer the Holy Ghost, and that because of the Restoration of the gospel, men on earth have that power today.

Who can say enough about the Holy Ghost? Who can put a value on having a member of the Godhead to give us comfort, peace, and inspiration? The privilege of the companionship of the Spirit is beyond generous, beyond amazing, beyond priceless. Imagine, each member of the Church has access to infinite intelligence! Perhaps this is why Joseph Smith called it the "unspeakable gift of the Holy Ghost" (D&C 121:26). And perhaps this is why Moroni gave it such emphasis as he completed the Book of Mormon.

The Holy Ghost Is a Companion

Several years after Joseph Smith was martyred, he appeared to President Brigham Young. Imagine that! Joseph Smith, now in the spirit world, must have known more than he ever knew on earth. And what one thing did he communicate to Brigham Young? His message for Brigham and for the Saints constitutes the theme of this chapter:

> Tell the people to be humble and faithful, and *be sure to keep the spirit of the Lord* and it will lead them right. Be careful and not turn away the small still voice; it will teach them what to do and where to go; it will yield the fruits of the Kingdom. . . . Tell the brethren that if they will follow the spirit of the Lord, they will go right. (*Teachings of Presidents of the Church: Brigham Young* [1997], 41; emphasis added)

Remember, when Moroni wrote these chapters he was alone. He mentioned that twice in Mormon 8 when he took over the responsibilities of compiling and completing the record from his father. Thus, the importance of the companionship of the Holy Ghost for the lone man Moroni cannot be overstated.

The Holy Ghost Is a "Warning Light"

A faithful companion will reassure you when you are doing well and won't be afraid to warn you when you are on the wrong track. Elder Gary E. Stevenson commented on these varying roles when he stated, "The Holy Ghost warns, the Holy Ghost comforts, and the Holy Ghost testifies" ("How Does the Holy Ghost Help You?" *Ensign*, May 2017, 120).

Have you ever had the "check engine" light in your car suddenly illuminate? I have. That can be an alarming experience. I didn't pull over soon enough, and as a result I "threw a rod," as the mechanics say, and had to purchase a new engine. We call these dashboard trouble indicators "warning lights." A warning light tells us that something is wrong, that there is a potential for trouble, and that we need to stop, identify, and fix the problem. Consider these two words together more slowly: *warning light*. A warning based on light and truth. The Holy Ghost is a "warning light" (or, in the tone of the scriptures, "a light of warning"). If one of us were about to step off a cliff that we didn't see coming, how grateful would we be for a friend to call out, "Stop!" "Don't go there!" or "That's the wrong way!" That's what a faithful companion would do.

The Holy Ghost is the type of friend who loves us enough to tell us when something is wrong, when we've done something wrong, or when we are about to. Some mortal friends may be too timid to warn us of a danger we don't see, but the Holy Ghost is not. Many have sat in Church meetings and, as the presence of the Spirit increases, have felt both inspired and scolded at the same time—I know I have, on many occasions. President Henry B. Eyring taught, "When you hear his voice by the Spirit you will always feel that you are impelled to do something. You mustn't be surprised if the instruction seems accompanied with what you feel as a rebuke" ("To Draw Closer to God," *Ensign*, May 1991, 67).

The warnings of the Spirit are always based on a desire to protect you from something, perhaps to protect you from persisting in a behavior that is hurtful to yourself or others. This dual role of chastising and inviting was stated beautifully by Elder Neal A.

Maxwell, who observed that "when conscience calls to us from the next ridge, it is not solely to scold but also to beckon" ("Notwithstanding My Weakness," *Ensign*, November 1976, 14).

The Holy Ghost Is a Tutor

Having the Spirit with us is also like being in the presence of a wise teacher—the wisest teacher, in fact. Elder Larry R. Lawrence spoke of His willingness to lead us. "However," he said, "we need to ask the Lord for directions along the way. We have to ask some difficult questions, like 'What do I need to change?' 'How can I improve?' 'What weakness needs strengthening?'"

President Harold B. Lee once suggested that each of us, using the same words as the rich young ruler, must ask the Lord, "What lack I yet?"(Matthew 19:20). How wonderful to know that the specialized, personal tutoring from the Holy Ghost will come when requested. Elder Lawrence went on to give three interesting examples of how the Holy Ghost will guide individuals when humbly invited:

Example One

I knew a faithful mother who humbled herself and asked, "What is keeping me from progressing?" In her case, the response from the Spirit came immediately: "Stop complaining." This answer surprised her; she had never thought of herself as a complainer. However, the message from the Holy Ghost was very clear. In the days that followed, she became conscious of her habit of complaining. Grateful for the prompting to improve, she determined to count her blessings instead of her challenges. Within days, she felt the warm approval of the Spirit.

Example Two

A humble young man who couldn't seem to find the right young woman went to the Lord for help: "What is keeping me from being the right man?" he asked. This answer came into his mind and heart: "Clean up your language." At that moment, he realized that several crude expressions had become part of his vocabulary, and he committed to change.

Example Three

A single sister bravely asked the question: "What do I need to change?" and the Spirit whispered to her, "Don't interrupt people when they are talking." The Holy Ghost really does give customized counsel. He is a completely honest companion and will tell us things that no one else knows or has the courage to say. ("What Lack I Yet?" *Ensign*, November 2015, 33–34)

Moroni was not alone, and neither are we. We have a "completely honest companion" in the Holy Ghost. What a blessing, for Moroni and for every latter-day traveler as well.

The rich young ruler in Matthew was perhaps a little overconfident when he asked, "What lack I yet?" Many of us would rather avoid that question, since we know that without any help we could fill a yellow pad or two with what we "lack." Even Nephi once lamented, "O wretched man that I am" (2 Nephi 4:17; wouldn't we love to be as "wretched" as Nephi?). Our question, rather than being stumped about what we might improve, might be more like, "Am I doing *anything* right?" or "Am I even close to becoming what I'm supposed to become?"

If we already feel overwhelmed with a sense of our weakness and weaknesses, perhaps we might approach the Lord with this question: "What *one thing* could I improve upon that would make the biggest difference?"

Thankfully, the Holy Ghost is a tender tutor. If we ask, He will teach us. His purpose is not to drown us by sending a flood of reminders of our weaknesses. But in the spirit of "line upon line, precept upon precept" (D&C 98:12), He might tell us one essential thing we can work on. He's called the Comforter, after all. He is not called the Scolder or the Guilt-Tripper. Neither is He the Accuser or Slanderer—those titles belong to Satan. The Holy Ghost is a loving tutor.

The Holy Ghost Is a Sword

The Apostle Paul described the armor of God to the Ephesians, giving a list of combat apparel constituting protection for the various parts of the body (see Ephesians 6). Thus, the shield of faith, the breastplate of righteousness, and other elements become our defense against the attacks of the world. But what about our offense? Interestingly, the final item mentioned on Paul's list (placed last to give it maximum emphasis) is not a defensive shield or a cover for some part of the body, but our one and only offensive weapon. Elder Jeffrey R. Holland explained:

> The scriptural passage speaks of breast-plates and shields and helmets, all of which are

important and protective but which leave us, in a sense, without an actual weapon yet. Are we to be only on the defensive? Are we to simply ward off blows and see it through and never be able, spiritually speaking, to strike a blow? No. We are supposed to advance in this and win a battle that started in heaven long ago. So we need some kind of even chance on the offense, and we are given it. You are given it. The weapon that is mentioned, the thing that allows us to actually do battle with the "darkness of the world," to use Paul's phrase, is "the sword of the Spirit, which is the word of God." May I repeat that? "The sword of the spirit, which is the word of God." ("Therefore, What?" 2000 New Testament Conference, Brigham Young University, August 8, 2000, 2)

While critics often ridicule religion as a "crutch" for the weak, Paul describes the Spirit as a sword. And yes, we may need to lean on our swords once in a while, but the battle goes on, and each item of our protective armor is accompanied by the sword of the Spirit, our weapon on offense, which allows us to actually "do battle" with the world.

The Holy Ghost Is a Protector

We spend a lot of time explaining to youth the standards of the gospel regarding movies, media, music, technology, clothing, language, and so forth. The most current *For the Strength of Youth* pamphlet is forty-six pages long. If we were to reduce those forty-six pages to seven words, they might be, "Don't do things that offend the Spirit." As a teacher, I love to see the look on the faces of the young people as it dawns on them that *every* standard, rule, and guideline in the pamphlet, *every one*, is about keeping the Holy Ghost with them.

Sometimes, someone might counter: "Well, that movie, that show, that type of depiction doesn't offend me." However, that's not the standard. It's not about what offends *you*—it's about what offends the *Holy Ghost*. And since we have each made a covenant to so live that we can "always have his Spirit to be with [us]" (Moroni 4:3), we have made a covenant not to offend the Holy Ghost by our choice of media.

I like to illustrate the connection between the rules and the doctrines by showing a picture of a tree. From a distance, most of what you see is leaves. But leaves are not just floating in the air. They are supported by branches, which in turn are supported by a trunk and roots. In the same way, the rules are not just arbitrary, random ideas intended to control behavior; they are supported by principles—*true* principles, which come from true doctrine. For example, a rule such as, "Don't participate in entertainment that is vulgar, immoral, inappropriate, or pornographic" is based upon the principle, "Whatever you look at has an effect on you." And the principle is founded in and supported by the doctrine, "Keep the Holy Ghost." The rules of the gospel have been articulated in different ways, but the doctrine of the gospel remains constant. It forms the roots of the gospel.

What strategy might Satan employ to destroy us? Just as a police officer's first command to a criminal suspect would be "Drop your weapon," the adversary will try to get us to drop ours. He would want to tempt us to do things that would cause us to relinquish our weapon, our sword, our protection—or, in other words, to lose the Holy Ghost. Once we have lost the Spirit, we are totally defensive. We are not as wise, we make poorer decisions, and we become weaker in our resolve to do right. Isn't it wonderful, then, that every week we can attend sacrament meeting and hear the priests place us under covenant that if we keep the Lord's commandments and always remember Him, we can always have His Spirit to be with us? That we can always be spiritually armed? Indeed, the Holy Ghost is a protector, a protection the Lord wants us to have.

Picture the Holy Ghost Being with You

We speak so often in rather abstract terms about "keeping the Spirit," "teaching by the Spirit," and "having the Spirit with us," but how do we actually do that? Are there any practical suggestions? Is it really possible to "always" have the Spirit with us, as promised in the sacrament prayers? I have always loved the experience related by Sister Wendy Watson (Nelson) when she was a marriage and family therapist at BYU. Sister Watson (Nelson) conducted a fascinating experiment with a group of women over a period of two weeks. The women were instructed that:

> For five days in their morning prayers, they were to pray with concerted effort for the Holy Ghost to be with them that day. Then, throughout the day, as they encountered any difficult, tempting, or trying situation, they were to pray

for and really picture the Spirit being right there with them.

"The experiences of these women," Dr. Watson (Nelson) reported, "blew us all away." Among the results they experienced were:

- An increased desire to dejunk their physical environments
- A greatly reduced desire to watch TV
- An increased desire to reach out to others and to follow through on commitments
- An increased ability to be kinder, gentler, and more patient
- An increased desire to take care of their bodies by living the Lord's law of health more fully
- An increased ability to see how they could have handled situations better
- An increased mental focus
- An increased ability and desire to really study and learn
- Old habits of backbiting, gossiping, and cynicalness falling away
- A dramatic increase in their physical

energy, because energy-draining negative
emotions were gone

- An unbelievable reduction in stress
- Profound changes in their conversations
  with others. (*Let Your Spirit Take the Lead*,
  CD [2004])

All of these wonderful results, a veritable spiritual
wish list, were accomplished because these women
prayed for and really believed the Spirit was with them.
They focused on the reality of that divine companionship, and it changed them in powerful ways. There's
not a personal success coach in the world who could
give you all that, and in only five days! Thankfully, you
don't need to hire a $500-an-hour life coach. You al-
ready have one, and it didn't cost you $500 an hour. It
was a gift you received at baptism.

The Privilege of the Holy Ghost

Yes, it really is possible to have the Spirit with us
always. It must be possible, because it is what the Lord
has promised. *Possible*, however, does not mean *easy* or
automatic. The promise stated in the sacrament prayer
is "that they *may* always have his Spirit to be with

them," not that they *will* always have His presence. President Brigham Young taught:

> There is no doubt, if a person lives according to the revelations given to God's people, he may have the Spirit of the Lord to signify to him His will, and to guide and to direct him in the discharge of his duties, in his temporal as well as his spiritual exercises. I am satisfied, however, that in this respect, we live far beneath our privileges. (*Journal of Discourses*, 26 vols. [1854–86], 12:105)

"Living beneath our privileges" is a phrase that is both sobering and motivating. President Dieter F. Uchtdorf shared a memorable story of a man on a Mediterranean cruise who learned this principle the hard way:

> He saved every penny until he had enough for his passage. Since money was tight, he brought an extra suitcase filled with cans of beans, boxes of crackers, and bags of powdered lemonade, and that is what he lived on every day.
>
> He would have loved to take part in the many activities offered on the ship—working out in

the gym, playing miniature golf, and swimming in the pool. He envied those who went to movies, shows, and cultural presentations. And, oh, how he yearned for only a taste of the amazing food he saw on the ship—every meal appeared to be a feast! But the man wanted to spend so very little money that he didn't participate in any of these. He was able to see the cities he had longed to visit, but for the most part of the journey, he stayed in his cabin and ate only his humble food.

On the last day of the cruise, a crew member asked him which of the farewell parties he would be attending. It was then that the man learned that not only the farewell party but almost everything on board the cruise ship—the food, the entertainment, all the activities—had been included in the price of his ticket. Too late the man realized that he had been living far beneath his privileges. ("Your Potential, Your Privilege," *Ensign*, May 2011, 58)

During this very time when Mormon and Moroni were watching the downfall of their people, it is interesting and informative that Mormon described their demise in terms of the Holy Ghost: "I fear lest the Spirit of the Lord hath ceased striving with them" (Moroni 9:4).

The gift of the Holy Ghost is a privilege, an "unspeakable" privilege, a privilege to live up to. Keeping the companionship of the Spirit ought to be the first item on everyone's daily "to-do" list. Sister Julie B. Beck once said that "the ability to qualify for, receive, and act on personal revelation is the single most important skill that can be acquired in this life" ("'And upon the Handmaids in Those Days Will I Pour Out My Spirit,'" *Ensign*, May 2010, 11). This is the quest to always have His Spirit to be with us.

Although we have had the privilege of the gift *conferred* upon us, it doesn't mean we have *received* it. When the gift of the Holy Ghost is given, the person conferring the gift uses the words, "Receive the Holy Ghost." He does not say, "Now the Holy Ghost will come upon you whether you want it or not," but "*Receive* the Holy Ghost." This means we have to desire it, to want it, and to let it in as we would receive a guest into our home. In other words, we have to live up to the privilege.

Moroni knew of the privilege of the Holy Ghost,

and he felt it important enough to devote precious space on the plates to teach future generations.

LIKENING MORONI
Moroni 2

I will receive the Holy Ghost

I will recognize that I am never really alone

I will trust the Holy Ghost as my warning light, my tutor, my weapon, and my protector

Chapter Seven

MORONI 3
"Disciples . . . Ordained Priests and Teachers"

How fascinating to see what Moroni has covered so far! Having shared with us his own tragic situation and his determination to rely on Christ, Moroni gives us a powerful second witness for Christ, stresses the importance of staying away from our enemies, and teaches us about keeping the Holy Ghost. What will he teach us next?

Moroni wants us to know that the priesthood organization existed and operated in the ancient Church. The priesthood was in their midst, and it blessed all their lives, as priesthood is intended to do. (The terms *priests* and *teachers* in the Book of Mormon do not refer to Aaronic Priesthood offices, but to the roles of those who held the higher priesthood; see 2 Nephi 6:2 and footnote 2a.)

We remember that after Moses led the children of Israel out of Egyptian bondage, the lands were divided among the different tribes: Reuben, Simeon, Judah, Issachar, and so forth. However, those of the tribe of Levi did not receive a land for their inheritance. Why? Because Levites were the only ones who held the priesthood, and they were not to live by themselves in one spot but to be divided among all the children of Israel to bless them and serve them. In the same way, the Lord has arranged it so that the priesthood is in our midst, and the ordinances and blessings of the priesthood are available to all of us, whether we personally hold the priesthood or not.

What Can We Do without Priesthood?

Perhaps one of the most often repeated verses in the Book of Mormon is 2 Nephi 25:23, "For we know that it is by grace that we are saved, after all we can do." There has been much helpful discussion about this verse in recent years as we continue to place it and understand it in the context of other scriptures and teachings. One interesting question to ask is, "What can we, by ourselves, do?" For example, can we be baptized by ourselves? No, we need the Lord's priesthood and an authorized priesthood holder. Can we be confirmed by ourselves? No again. We need the Lord's priesthood and a priesthood holder. Can we receive the Holy Ghost by ourselves? No once again. What exactly can we, *by ourselves*, do? This is an especially interesting question when we remember Jesus' statement, "I am the vine, ye are the branches . . . without me *ye can do nothing*" (John 15:5; emphasis added). Yet another interesting verse to bring into the discussion involves the conversion of a certain group of Lamanites who expressed:

> Since it has been *all that we could do* (as we were the most lost of all mankind) to repent of all our sins and the many murders which we have committed, and to get God to take them away from our hearts, for it was *all we could do* to repent sufficiently before God that he would take away our stain. (Alma 24:11; emphasis added)

In this verse, "all they could do" by themselves was repent—or, in other words, turn their hearts toward and yield their agency to God. And, of course, repentance itself is only possible because of God. So, while

63

some critics of our theology may think that we believe we are earning our salvation by our good works, or by "all we can do," we can see that, actually, we need the Lord and His grace and His priesthood from the very beginning, and not "after" anything.

This is a larger topic for another time and place, but for our purposes here, we see the blessing of having the priesthood and priesthood keys in our midst. Without them, the first ordinances of the gospel would not be available (see Articles of Faith 1:4). We could not be baptized or receive the Holy Ghost, and we could not renew our covenants at the sacrament table after baptism.

Elder Dallin H. Oaks taught that "Priesthood power blesses all of us. Priesthood keys direct women as well as men, and priesthood ordinances and priesthood authority pertain to women as well as men" ("The Keys and Authority of the Priesthood," *Ensign*, May 2014, 49).

The priesthood is both a blessing and a burden, as is being a member of the house of Israel. Being a chosen people does not mean being chosen to sit on a throne and be admired. It's more like being chosen to mow the lawn or to bring in the harvest. Being chosen means being chosen to work! Doing the work of the Lord is refining and humbling. My mission president used to say, "The Lord gets His work done through the people, and He gets His people 'done' through the work."

Moroni, having briefly told us that priests and teachers were ordained, proceeds to tell us one of the most important reasons why in the next two chapters.

LIKENING MORONI
Moroni 3

I acknowledge the blessings of
the priesthood in my midst

I value the priesthood and the ordinances
and blessings it makes available

Chapter Eight

MORONI 4–5
"Administering the Flesh and Blood of Christ"

Moroni, having mentioned that the priesthood existed among the Nephites anciently, now proceeds to tell us one of the reasons why. For Moroni to engrave the sacrament prayers on the plates is a testimony that the sacrament was an essential, not an optional, part of their worship.

Some have wondered why the sacrament prayers appear in both the Book of Mormon and the Doctrine and Covenants. Perhaps one reason is to impress upon us the consistency of the doctrine. After the Savior's Atonement, a major part of the worship of the house of Israel immediately ceased. As Elder Bruce R. McConkie put it, "Sacrifice stopped, and sacrament started" (*Doctrinal New Testament Commentary*, 3 vols.

[1965–73], 1:79), and the sacrament has been a part of true worship ever since. The fact that the same prayers appear in the Doctrine and Covenants shows that the Nephites didn't invent the prayers or develop their own practices of worship, but that those prayers were revealed to them in their day, "according to the commandments of Christ" (Moroni 4:1), just as they have been revealed to us again in ours.

We are counseled against using visual aids in sacrament meeting talks, yet one of the most powerful visual aids is bolted to the floor in the front of every chapel. The sacrament table is a reminder of the Savior's mercy, His forgiveness, and, of course, His selfless sacrifice for us. It can remind us of both a table for sharing a meal (like the Last Supper) and also an altar for sacrifice, or the "table of the Lord," as Malachi called it (Malachi 1:7).

My friend Kim Petersen, an institute teacher in southern Utah, commented that on one occasion he entered the chapel and saw the sacrament table with its white cloth covering the bread and water trays. For a moment, he said, it almost resembled a body covered by a cloth, a great reminder of the sacrifice of Jesus' body and blood, which the sacrament represents.

His comment has blessed my life and made me look more reverently toward the front of the chapel as I enter. The sacrament table does not reside in a storage room where it can be wheeled in and dusted off for Christmas and Easter; it is a permanent and weekly part of our worship.

Moroni's inspired inclusion of the sacrament prayers gives us the opportunity to examine each prayer more closely and to look for depth and meaning in each phrase. As we ponder what might be most important to the Lord, we might ponder the things He has asked us to repeat. Although we are baptized only once, our recommitment to our baptismal covenants is performed weekly through the sacrament. Although we receive our temple endowment only once, as we return to the temple to act as proxy for others, we remember our covenants and promised blessings.

Brother Gary Poll suggested that if Heavenly Father had a favorite scripture, He might arrange it so that His people would hear it often, so that the person uttering the scripture might be kneeling, and so that all listening would have their eyes closed. What is in these prayers Moroni recorded that is so important and so timeless?

"O God, the Eternal Father." Would you like to hear something interesting? Guess how many times the phrase *Eternal Father* appears in the King James Bible? Zero. Not once. (The phrase *Everlasting Father* appears in Isaiah 9:6, but it is referring to Christ.) Interestingly, *Eternal Father* appears thirteen times in the Book of Mormon. We believe that God really is our Father in Heaven, that He is eternally our Father, and, in the sacrament prayers, we address Him as such. Our first article of faith states, "We believe in God, the Eternal Father, and in His Son, Jesus Christ, and in the Holy Ghost." In the sacrament prayers, we address the Eternal Father, the Father of the spirits of all men (see Hebrews 12:9), and the Father of Jesus Christ.

"We ask thee in the name of thy Son, Jesus Christ." Jesus is our advocate with the Father. He told the Nephites, "Ye must always pray unto the Father in my name" (3 Nephi 18:19). In keeping with the Savior's instructions, we offer this prayer, and all other prayers, to our Heavenly Father, in the name of Jesus Christ.

"To bless and sanctify this bread." We may recall that Jesus fed five thousand with loaves and fishes, and many in the multitude followed Him in hopes that he would feed them again. The next day, Jesus spoke to those who sought Him during the night. They asked Him if He was going to be like Moses, since Moses gave them manna. Jesus replied, "Moses didn't give you the manna." He continued (my paraphrase), "Your fathers ate manna and they are all dead. I could give you bread that, if you ate it, you would never die." Their response was, not surprisingly, "Lord, evermore give us this bread. And Jesus said unto them, I am the bread of life: he that cometh to me shall never hunger; and he that believeth on me shall never thirst" (see John 6:34–35). In this context, it is interesting to remember that the word *Bethlehem* means "house of bread," which of course is Jesus' birthplace.

"To the souls of all those who partake of it." When we bless our food or refreshments, we often use the wording "to nourish and strengthen our *bodies*." But blessing the sacrament to our souls is different. Jesus said if we ate of the bread of life, we would never hunger again! Clearly, He was talking about bread for the soul, or for the spirit and body together. The scriptures teach that "the spirit and the body are the soul of man" (D&C 88:15). Thus, the manna of the Old Testament was sent to nourish and strengthen bodies, but the bread of life of the New Testament is for the nourishment of body and spirit, or, in other words, for the soul. Jesus taught the Nephites, "He that eateth this bread eateth of my body to his soul; and he that drinketh of this wine drinketh of my blood to his soul; and his soul shall never hunger nor thirst, but shall be filled" (3 Nephi 20:8).

"That they may eat in remembrance of the body of thy Son." Each Sunday, when I hear the priest use the words "in remembrance of the body of thy Son," my favorite thing to "remember" is the empty tomb. Because Jesus rose again, we will all rise again. My parents always taught me that I was supposed to think about Jesus during the sacrament. Sometimes I wasn't sure what to think about. Today, my favorite thing to remember about Jesus' body is that it was gone when the disciples came to the tomb. In the words of the angel, "He is not here: for he is risen, as he said" (Matthew 28:6).

"And witness unto thee, O God, the Eternal Father, that they are willing to take upon them the name of thy Son." What does "take upon them" mean? Well, when you were born, your parents gave you a name. When you're *born again*, you take upon yourself

71

the name of Christ. When you covenant to live the life of a disciple of Christ, it's as if you're saying, "Hey, everyone, do you want to see what Latter-day Saints are all about? Watch me. Do you want to see how we treat people, even those who can't do us any good? Watch me. Do you want to see what kind of movies we see and how we talk and dress? Watch me." At times, we might be tempted to say, "I'm trying, but don't watch me too closely!" We are all imperfect, which is why we return to the sacrament table week after week.

Elder Dallin H. Oaks gave us a call to action when he taught that the name of Christ might also mean the work of Christ:

> What does the name of Christ and that covenant mean? The most frequent single meaning of the scriptures that refer to the name of the Lord seem to mean the work of the Lord, His work, His atonement, His mission. . . . Everyone who covenants that they are willing to take upon them the name of Christ is saying, "I will handle my share of that great mission, and my share is what I am called to do." (April 2015 Training Meeting on the Sabbath and the Sacrament)

Look at the front cover of your scriptures. Is your

name embossed there? If so, we might say that your scriptures have "taken your name upon them." What does that mean? It means those scriptures belong to you. In the same way, when we take upon us the name of Christ, we belong to Him. The Lord told Alma the Elder, "Blessed is this people who are willing to bear my name; for in my name shall they be called; and they are mine" (Mosiah 26:18). It's nice to know that when we put His name on us, we belong to Him.

Sister Jean A. Stevens taught:

> Covenants with God help us to know who we really are. They connect us to Him in a personal way through which we come to feel our value in His sight and our place in His kingdom. In a way we can't fully comprehend, we are known and loved individually by Him. ("Covenant Daughters of God," *Ensign*, November 2014, 115)

"And always remember him." *Remember* is a very important word. President Spencer W. Kimball taught:

> When you look in the dictionary for the most important word, do you know what it is? It could be "remember." Because all of you have made covenants—you know what to do and you know

73

how to do it—our greatest need is to remember. That is why everyone goes to sacrament meeting every Sabbath day—to take the sacrament and listen to the priests pray that they "may always remember him and keep his commandments which he has given them." Nobody should ever forget to go to sacrament meeting. "Remember" is the word. "Remember is the program" ("Circles of Exaltation," in *Charge to Religious Educators*, 2nd ed. [1982], 12)

It's interesting how often the Book of Mormon uses the word *remember*. It uses *remember* to describe the righteous: "Yea, they did remember how great things the Lord had done for them" (Alma 62:50). And it uses *remember* to describe the wicked: "Ye are swift to do iniquity but slow to remember the Lord your God" (1 Nephi 17:45). Next time you go through the Book of Mormon, watch for the word *remember* and its opposite, *forget*—you'll be impressed!

"And keep his commandments which he hath given them." Jesus taught, "If ye love me, keep my commandments" (John 14:15). Keeping all the commandments is a pretty tall order. For mortal and fallen man, it's impossible. But that is exactly why we take the sacrament so often. Brother Stephen E. Robinson taught:

> In many denominations, it would be thought odd that the sacrament of the Lord's Supper is offered every week. Yet Latter-day Saints know that imperfect beings must regularly reaffirm their personal goal of perfection, being justified in the meantime by the atonement of Christ. Accordingly, each week we come before the Lord as we prepare for the sacrament and say essentially, "Heavenly Father, I wasn't perfect again this week, but I repent of my sins and reaffirm my commitment to keep all the commandments. I promise to go back and try again with all my heart, might, mind, and strength. I still want and need the cleansing that comes through faith, repentance, and baptism. Please extend my contract, my covenant of baptism, and grant me the continued blessings of the Atonement and the companionship of the Holy Ghost." (*Believing Christ: The Parable of the Bicycle and Other Good News* [1992], 52)

"That they may always have his Spirit to be with them. Amen." Near the conclusion of Jesus' visit with the righteous Nephites and Lamanites, the multitude of 2500 looked upon Jesus as if asking Him to tarry with them, but Jesus told them He couldn't stay: "Behold, my time is at hand," He said, and "now I go unto the Father" (3 Nephi 17:1, 4).

We don't know what kind of time constraints pressed upon the Savior of the world, but Jesus assured the multitude that although He couldn't stay personally, they could always have His Spirit to be with them through partaking of the sacrament (see 3 Nephi 18:7,11). Elder Bruce C. Hafen observed that the promise was first made not in the words of a prayer uttered by a priest, but in the Savior's own voice:

> In introducing the sacrament to the Nephites, Christ said, "And if ye do always remember me ye shall have my spirit to be *with you*" (3 Nephi 18:11). So Christ first spoke the sacrament prayer as He personally taught what the sacrament is. And the promised "with you" is more than a formal prayer; it is His voice, speaking His promise of constant companionship to each of us. (*Spiritually Anchored in Unsettled Times* [2009], 34)

For each of us in our time
ally in his, our feelings of be
His promise of always be.
like Elder Neal A. Maxwell on
the sacrament to himself and felt u.
panionship of the Lord. Interestingly, wh.
Neal A. Maxwell crouched alone in a foxhole i.
home, another boy on the same island also struggi.
to survive, but the Lord was "with them," and His eyes
were upon them both. Elder Maxwell later reported:

> Unknown to me then was how the ravages of
> the battle on Okinawa were affecting an eight-
> year-old Okinawan boy, Kensei Nagamine. His fa-
> ther and brother were killed in the Battle of Shuri,
> and his pregnant mother was able to take her five
> children, including this youthful son, to the north
> end of the island and comparative safety, even as
> they were repeatedly machine gunned by fighter
> planes many times. Though unaware, an eigh-
> teen- and an eight-year-old were then only miles
> apart. Many years later we met; by then he was
> the president of the Okinawa Stake. It was my
> privilege later on (after his tour as stake president)
> to call him as patriarch to the Okinawa Stake. He

w President Nagamine of the Tokyo temple!
rely the Lord had His eyes upon him long ago!
(*One More Strain of Praise* [1999], 105)

What a comfort to think of the sacrament as a divine answer to loneliness and a reminder that His eyes are upon all of His children.

Moroni 5—Prayer on the Wine or the Water

Many of the words and phrases used in the prayer on the bread are also used in the prayer on the wine, or water, so we won't repeat them here. But why are there two prayers? Perhaps because the sacrifice of Jesus' body and Jesus' blood symbolize different things, and they accomplish different things. For example, symbolically speaking, our sins are not cleansed by Jesus' body but by His blood. One scripture that we don't normally connect to the sacrament, but that can teach us about the roles of Jesus' body and blood, is Moses 1:39:

> For behold, this is my work and my glory—to bring to pass the immortality and eternal life of man.

To most people, immortality and eternal life might sound like the same thing, but they're not.

The difference between immortality and eternal life coincides perfectly with the different emblems of the sacrament.

BREAD—JESUS' BODY—IMMORTALITY

WATER—JESUS' BLOOD—ETERNAL LIFE

Because of Jesus' body, we will all be resurrected—that's immortality. And that has already been accomplished for everyone. Because of Jesus' blood, which is sometimes spoken of as a "cleanser," we have the possibility of eternal life. Moroni taught:

> O then ye unbelieving, turn ye unto the Lord; cry mightily unto the Father in the name of Jesus, that perhaps ye may be found spotless, pure, fair, and white, having been *cleansed by the blood of the Lamb*, at that great and last day. (Mormon 9:6; emphasis added)

Eternal life is not the same as immortality, or living forever. The word *eternal* refers to a quality of life as well as a duration of life, since "Eternal" is one of God's names (see D&C 19:6–12). Everyone will enjoy immortality, but because of the shedding of Jesus' blood, we may be forgiven, cleansed, and changed so that we may enjoy eternal life, the kind of life that God leads.

Another interesting difference in the two prayers involves the covenant of remembering. When the priests bless the bread, the prayer says that we are "*willing* to . . . always remember him." In the prayer on the water, however, we witness that we "*do* always remember him," a definite step up in our commitment to remembering Christ.

Past, Present, and Future

Moroni 4 and 5 teach us the importance of the sacrament. While the sacrament looks to the past in remembering Jesus' sacrifice, it also promises His Spirit in the present, and it points to a glorious future. Imagine how important and comforting the sacrament might have been to Moroni as a symbol and promise of renewal, restoration, resurrection, and Christ's overcoming spiritual and physical death for each of us and our families. As we contemplate being reunited with our loved ones because of Jesus' resurrection, we might suppose that Moroni also thought of his loved ones and their reunion made possible by Christ. Moroni had lost nearly everything, but he didn't lose his faith.

We often speak of the justice and mercy of God, and if we had to choose one of these traits over the other, we would probably all say mercy is our favorite. But we should not overlook the upside of justice! Many times in life, we lose things, we suffer losses, and we endure injustices. Many of these emotional, physical, and family losses come through no fault of our own, but through the misuse of agency on the part of other people. Would a God of justice not see the unfairness in such cases? Would He not see our suffering as unjust when it was brought upon us by the poor choices of others? I love the statement of the Prophet Joseph Smith, who boldly assured:

> All your losses will be made up to you in the resurrection, provided you continue faithful. By the vision of the Almighty I have seen it. (*Teachings of Presidents of the Church: Joseph Smith* [2007], 51)

We have a family friend who has endured many trials and difficulties in this life, not of her own making. She was given an inspired blessing wherein she was told that while she might not see justice in this life, justice would be applied in the next. It gave her great comfort and helped her completely let go of the desire for vengeance, allowing her to feel the healing influence of the Savior and move on.

Isn't it wonderful that the Lord can be merciful and just at the same time? We worship a God whom we can trust completely, a God who exercises these principles with perfect balance and harmony.

The sacrament prayers take less than a minute to utter, but they can be pondered for a lifetime. Moroni etched them in gold to remind us of the importance of staying in covenant with Christ.

LIKENING MORONI
Moroni 4–5

I will renew my covenants often by partaking of the sacrament

I will remember the Savior's sacrifice

I strive to be worthy of the promise of His companionship

I look forward with hope to the restoration and resurrection made possible by the Savior

Chapter Nine

MORONI 6
"Numbered Among the
. . . Church of Christ"

Having taught us about the Savior, the Holy Ghost, the priesthood, and the sacrament, Moroni continues by teaching us what follows—participation in a church.

The strait and narrow path is a commonly used and widely understood biblical metaphor (see Matthew 7:14). Interestingly, the Book of Mormon adds a gate, a rod of iron, substantial hazards, and boisterous opposition to those traveling on the strait and narrow (see 1 Nephi 8–15). Nephi teaches that the path so often talked about is accessed by a gate:

> The gate by which ye should enter is repentance and baptism by water; and then cometh a remission of your sins by fire and by the Holy

Ghost. And then are ye in this strait and narrow path which leads to eternal life. (2 Nephi 31:17–18)

Passing through the gate signifies entrance onto the path, or into the kingdom of God on earth. In the nine verses of Moroni 6, Moroni shares with us a few essential practices of the ancient Saints in the New World. By implication, Moroni is showing us the value of a church! While some in the Christian world may disagree, we believe that Jesus did in fact ordain leaders, bestow keys, and organize a church through which His people would teach and strengthen one another. In this way, Moroni 6 is like a mini "Handbook of Instructions."

The Church of Imperfect Members

I have heard people say, "I don't believe in organized religion." I am tempted to respond, "Well, go visit the nursery, it's not that organized." Another one we've probably all heard is, "I'm spiritual, but not religious," whatever that means. Moroni's words and instructions, while giving us a model for modern worship, also serve to validate that there is a place and a purpose for organized religion.

Many years ago, I read an essay titled "Why the Church Is as True as the Gospel." In sharing our testimonies, we sometimes use the words *church* and *gospel* interchangeably. The author of this essay was trying to show that belonging to a church, with all of its administrative challenges and with its rolls bursting with imperfect people, is part of the test of mortality. The gospel message is true, as we all believe. But in a way, so is the church of imperfect people, because it is part of our test—a true test. In an address titled "Why the Church," Elder D. Todd Christofferson taught:

> In the Church we not only learn divine doctrine; we also experience its application. As the body of Christ, the members of the Church minister to one another in the reality of day-to-day life. All of us are imperfect; we may offend and be offended. We often test one another with our personal idiosyncrasies. In the body of Christ, we have to go beyond concepts and exalted words and have a real "hands-on" experience as we learn to "live together in love" [D&C 42:45]. (*Ensign*, November 2015, 108–9)

One Sunday, while serving as a bishop, I arose to conduct ward business, and I announced to the congregation that I had succeeded in transferring the membership records of all the perfect people out of our ward. "They have been moved to the Perfect First Ward in the Perfect Stake," I reported, "so from this point on, if anyone disappoints you, or if things don't run as smoothly as they should, you won't be surprised." I knew after my announcement there wouldn't be any more complaints, murmurings, or disgruntlements (wink, wink).

We Believe in Meetings

After people were baptized, Moroni reports, they were "numbered among the people of the church of Christ; and their names were taken, that they might be remembered and nourished by the good word of God" (Moroni 6:4). This brief and beautiful description offers another reason why we have a church. Within that phrase, we can see that the ancient Church maintained membership records and had some sort of system for keeping track of members. But Moroni wasn't finished—why do we keep these records and remember these people? "To keep them continually watchful unto prayer, relying alone upon the merits of Christ, who was the author and the finisher of their faith."

The Church is the vehicle to help keep us focused upon Christ and "nourished by the good word of God."

And how often do we meet in this church? Religious holidays only? Semiannually? Monthly? Not even close. We meet often. Sometimes multiple meetings per week. One might even say we meet "religiously." Which is why someone composed the tongue-in-cheek "fourteenth article of faith":

> We believe in meetings, we hope for meetings, we have endured many meetings, and we hope to be able to endure more meetings. If there is any justification for holding a meeting, we seek after these things . . .

Moroni reports that "the church did meet together oft, to fast and to pray, and to speak one with another concerning the welfare of their souls" (Moroni 6:5). Meeting together often gives us the opportunity to strengthen and be strengthened often. And what else do we do while we meet? Read it again: we "speak *one with another* concerning the welfare of [our] souls." Note that Moroni did not say that only one person would speak each week, but that we would speak "one with another."

Each of us has opportunities to teach and be

taught, which is one of the wonderful benefits of fellowship and a lay clergy. We take turns teaching and ministering and administering, and every few months we play "musical callings" when we release and sustain, and it becomes someone else's challenge and opportunity to serve in a place where he or she feels inadequate and unprepared. Sure, we experience the stress, but also the growth. The Lord expands our abilities and expands our spirits, and we find ourselves weeping at our release, only to find our heart pounding when our next new calling is issued. None of this would be possible if we sat at home in our recliners being "spiritual but not religious." Indeed, the Church is as true as the gospel.

We'd Like to Invite You to Church

Please notice, Moroni didn't begin these final ten chapters by talking about the Church and how they ran the Church. The Church organization and its operation was actually down the list a bit. He began by talking about Christ, then the Holy Ghost, then how we receive Christ and the Holy Ghost—and only then did be begin to talk about the Church. The sequence is inspired.

One evening many years ago, I set out with another priesthood brother to try to tie up loose ends in our membership records. Our entire quorum was organized into companionships to canvass the neighborhood and attempt to identify all these people on the rolls, update our records, and invite anyone we found to come to church. We dressed up in our church uniforms, shirt and tie, list in hand, and began to knock on doors. At one of our first houses, a young man greeted us coolly and said, "You must be new to this assignment; the person you're looking for doesn't want any contact from the Church." "Well," my companion asked politely, "could we at least ask you a question?" "No!" was the response, and the door was shut just shy of being slammed. Fortunately, some of the others in our group made contact with some who actually welcomed the visit, but even with the best of intentions, I have to admit our experience was less than positive.

I reflected often on that encounter, and it dawned on me that I should have applied what I had heard years earlier in a wonderfully insightful Education Week lecture by Dr. Stephen R. Covey, entitled "6 Events." He suggested that not only were the events of the Restoration of the gospel important, but *the order in which they came* was in fact a formula for solving life's problems (including bringing less-active members back to the Church). His presentation was absolutely fascinating. Here's a summary of the events and the corresponding "lessons":

EVENT	LESSON
1. The First Vision	"Who is God, and who am I?"
2. The Restoration of the Gospel (Translation of the Book of Mormon)	"Whose am I" (Jesus Christ died for me)
3. The Restoration of the Priesthood	"How can I receive Christ?"
4. The Restoration of the Church	"Where do I go to receive Christ?"
5. The Restoration of Keys of Salvation for Living and Dead	"What is the work I should do in this life?"
6. The Restoration of Temple Ordinances	"Why did God bring about the Restoration?"

Source: *6 Events: The Restoration Model for Solving Life's Problems* [2010], 224.

Notice that the first mention of "the Church" doesn't appear on the list until number four. Perhaps the mistake we had made, at least with the particular household involved, was that we were focusing too much on Lesson Four instead of Lesson One. Someone who has been away from the Church for a while may need to begin the learning and conversion process all over again.

Some years later, I was called to serve as bishop, and on one occasion, remembering that encounter a few years earlier, I left my shirt and tie in the closet, and I set out alone in my blue jeans and hoodie. I talked to some people on the porch of their apartment for some time. We talked about the weather, the neighborhood, and the garbage-collection schedule. Eventually (and I'll never forget the look on their faces), I told them I was the local bishop. And guess what? They didn't kick me off the porch or slam the door. They didn't tell me to get lost. In fact, we continued to talk about things for a while, and afterward, we exchanged smiles, and today I even receive a wave when they drive by. I began to refer to these more informal visits as "hoodie visits." They were much less intimidating to the residents than the approach of a couple of guys in shirts and ties. They also required some patience. Instead of skipping to Lesson Four and asking, "Hey, how come you don't come to church?" perhaps our first lesson should be, "I'm your neighbor," and, after some small talk and some neighborly contact and service (perhaps over an extended period of time), "By the way . . . did you know that God is real, and that He knows and loves you?" Delivering that message may require some patience.

The Church Provides Opportunities to Serve

We might remember Ammon, the son of King Mosiah, who was called to serve as a missionary among the Lamanites but who entered the land of Ishmael *deliberately incognito!* No one knew why he was there. Without revealing his mission, Ammon volunteered to be a servant to the king. Ammon thought to himself (slightly paraphrased), "I will win their hearts; then, I will lead them to believe in my words" (see Alma 17:29). An interesting sequence! As someone else once said describing the same idea, "We have to *warm* them before we *warn* them." My guess is that Ammon also left his shirt and necktie at home (those were the days). Most important, Ammon's motive was love and concern for his fellow man, not merely the desire to fulfill an assignment.

When Ammon was confronted by the servants of the king, and eventually bound and brought to stand before the king's throne, he was compelled to announce why he was there: "I will be thy servant," he declared, and serve he did (Alma 17:25). An additional and wonderful purpose of the Church organization is the opportunity for service. Elder D. Todd Christofferson also taught:

> This religion is not concerned only with self; rather, we are all called to serve. We are the eyes, hands, head, feet, and other members of the body of Christ, and even "those members . . . which seem to be more feeble, are necessary" [1 Corinthians 12:22]. We need these callings, and we need to serve. ("Why the Church," 109)

Throughout recorded history, people have wondered how best to serve God. Sincere people around the world have pursued different methods. How do we best serve God? Personal study? Personal prayers? Personal development? Should we hide away from the world in a remote fortress and study holy books?

(That has a certain appeal, doesn't it!) King Benjamin cleared it up when he taught:

> And behold, I tell you these things that ye may learn wisdom; that ye may learn that when ye are in the service of your fellow beings ye are only in the service of your God. (Mosiah 2:17)

The Church provides an environment for and opportunities for serving our fellow man. Fellowship is an element of the true Church, and we cannot enjoy the benefits of fellowship, and grow through the challenges of fellowship, if we are the only fellow on the ship. Serving each other *is* how we serve God.

What If I Don't Want to Be Rescued?

I once attended a leadership training meeting in which I heard a fascinating story by Elder Von G. Keetch. He had a conversation with a "search and rescue" specialist while on an airliner. This rescuer did much of his work on Mount Hood near Portland, Oregon. He said that usually by the time he found victims on the mountain, they didn't really want to be rescued. They were in a situation where they finally felt comfortable and warm as a result of hypothermia. In these cases, the rescuer knows what he must do.

First, he has to get the victims to trust him. He will introduce himself, talk about their hometowns, and win them over with some conversation. Second, he has to give them a task. Typically, he would use his satellite phone and have them call their loved ones and let them know they've been found. Finally, he has to raise their body temperature by giving them some warm nourishment, like hot cocoa.

Elder Keetch let that sink in for a minute, then asked us, "Did you hear that? If someone doesn't want to be rescued, what do you do? You give them a friend, a responsibility, and nourishment, exactly the approach President Gordon B. Hinckley taught us to take with new members."

The Great Privilege of Our Church

Although the Church is down the list at Lesson Four, its importance cannot be overstated. Jesus organized a church. Why? Why can't we just believe in Christ, try to follow Him in our personal conduct, and go our own way? The Church is a place for the keys of the priesthood to exist and for its ordinances to be given. A wonderful answer to the question of the purpose of the Church appears in D&C 84:19–21:

And this greater priesthood administereth the gospel and holdeth the key of the mysteries of the kingdom, even the key of the knowledge of God. Therefore, in the ordinances thereof, the power of godliness is manifest. And without the ordinances thereof, and the authority of the priesthood, the power of godliness is not manifest unto men in the flesh.

Moroni teaches us that no matter our trials and our circumstances, we stay on the strait and narrow path by remaining active in the kingdom of God on earth— or, in other words, the Church. If we don't attend church, we might as well not have one. As President Spencer W. Kimball taught, "We do not go to [church] to be entertained, or even solely to be instructed. We go to worship the Lord" ("The Sabbath—A Delight," *Ensign*, January 1978, 4–5). The Church and its members are not perfect, and although we might not feel the Spirit every time we attend, if we don't attend, we are less likely to feel the Spirit in other areas of our lives.

Sometimes we hear our brothers and sisters say, "I know the Church is true," and others might say, "I know the gospel is true." In either case, we know what they mean, and we rejoice in their testimony. The gospel, the Church, the priesthood, and the opportunities of fellowship are all elements of the kingdom of God on earth, and Moroni reminds us of our citizenship in the kingdom.

LIKENING MORONI
Moroni 6

I embrace organized religion

I am active in both the Church and the gospel

I am numbered and remembered, and I remember others by home and visiting teaching

I meet often with fellow Saints to remember the Savior and to discuss the welfare of my soul

I am nourished by the good word

Chapter Ten

MORONI 7
"I Show unto You
the Way to Judge"

In Moroni 7, Moroni teaches us about the "Spirit of Christ" or light of Christ, which is given to every man, and admonishes us to "search diligently in the light of Christ" as we are compelled to judge and make judgments. Working with people in an imperfect world and in an imperfect church will require us to make our best judgments, sometimes multiple judgments per day.

When I was a boy, my brother and I collected football cards. Sometimes mini posters came with the cards, which we unfolded and pasted on the closet door in the bedroom we shared. I still remember admiring the photos of quarterbacks Fran Tarkenton of the Vikings and Roman Gabriel of the Rams. I knew much more about the NFL and its players back then than I do now. As more and more football games were broadcast on TV, we noticed the fans sitting behind the goalposts holding aloft banners and signs with scripture references. It was their way of spreading the gospel, an "end-zone evangelism," we might say. Interestingly, the verse displayed most often was John 3:16: "For God so loved the world, that he gave his only begotten Son, that whosoever believeth in him should not perish, but have everlasting life"—a wonderful summary of the gospel, and arguably one of the most widely known Bible verses. At least it used to be. I believe that currently, the most widely quoted biblical phrase would be "judge not" (Matthew 7:1).

These days, it seems that anytime anyone makes a statement about values or morals, or tries to say "this is wrong," or "this is inappropriate," they will be countered, often aggressively and loudly, with something like, "Hey, you're judging! You can't do that! Jesus said don't judge." Well, in some contexts He did, and in others He told us we must judge. Which one is right?

Elder Dallin H. Oaks, who served as a Utah State Supreme Court judge before being called to serve as an Apostle, gave a wonderfully insightful and clarifying presentation called "'Judge Not' and Judging." In one of his introductory paragraphs, he said:

> I have been puzzled that some scriptures command us not to judge and others instruct us that we should judge and even tell us how to do it. But as I have studied these passages I have become convinced that these seemingly contradictory directions are consistent when we view them with the perspective of eternity. The key is to understand that there are two kinds of judging: final judgments, which we are forbidden to make, and intermediate judgments, which we are directed to make, but upon righteous principles. (*Ensign*, August 1999, 7)

Isn't it wonderful to know that we are relieved from making final judgments? We're off the hook! Have you ever tried to talk about the gospel with someone and had the person ask, "So, do you think I'm going to hell?" Now we know that we can answer, "How should I know? That's not my call. I don't know your background, circumstances, life experiences, or trials. A just and merciful God makes those judgments—I don't even touch 'em."

Intermediate judgments are a different story. Each

of us makes, and must make, and really cannot avoid making, hundreds of judgments every day. These are intermediate judgments. They might range from the simplest of decisions, such as choosing which route to take to go to work, to more important judgments, like how to spend our time when priorities compete between family and Church callings. Our children must make judgments involving whom to choose as friends, which social events to attend and which to avoid, and eventually whom to date and marry. Should they not judge very carefully in such cases?

If you were looking for someone to watch your kids, and you discovered one of the candidates had a criminal background, would you say to yourself, "Well, I shouldn't judge"? No, you would judge. Jesus commanded us to judge, but to judge righteously.

Moroni, quoting his father, Mormon, gave us a key to judge in such a way that our judgment would be as plain "as the daylight is from the dark night" (Moroni 7:15).

> But whatsoever thing persuadeth men to do evil, and believe not in Christ, and deny him, and serve not God, then ye may know with a perfect knowledge it is of the devil; for after this

manner doth the devil work, for he persuadeth no man to do good, no, not one; neither do his angels; neither do they who subject themselves unto him.

And now, my brethren, seeing that ye know the light by which ye may judge, which light is the light of Christ, see that ye do not judge wrongfully; for with that same judgment which ye judge ye shall also be judged. (Moroni 7:17–18)

In our dealings with our fellow Church members and with our fellow man in general, judging others in the kindest light possible is always best. Judging with a forgiving heart is always best. And when we do, we can expect that type of charity in return when we are judged.

Critics of the Church direct many of their attacks on Joseph Smith. If you want to find fault with Church leaders past and present, you can. And you will. What have you proven? That none of us is perfect. Congratulations, you've discovered what we already know. Joseph Smith himself said:

I told them I was but a man, and they must not expect me to be perfect; if they expected perfection from me, I should expect it from them; but if they would bear with my infirmities and the infirmities of the brethren, I would likewise bear with their infirmities. (*Teachings of Presidents of the Church: Joseph Smith* [2007], 522)

God works, and must work, through imperfect people, because no perfect people are available. Elder Jeffrey R. Holland taught: "Imperfect people are all God has ever had to work with. That must be terribly frustrating to Him, but He deals with it. So should we" ("Lord, I Believe," *Ensign*, May 2013, 94).

Recognizing our own imperfection will help us excuse it in others. "Well," we might say, "I'd forgive that person if they asked for it, but since they haven't, I'll wait." How does the Lord feel about that? Does He forgive us only when we ask? In this stunning statement of the Lord's mercy, Joseph Smith taught: "Should we even forgive our brother or our enemy before they ask it our heavenly father would be equally as merciful unto us" (*The Words of Joseph Smith: The Contemporary Accounts of the Nauvoo Discourses of the Prophet Joseph*, compiled and edited by Andrew F. Ehat and Lyndon W. Cook [1980], 7).

We too may become "terribly frustrated" with those

whom we deal with in our families, our work, and our ward, but perhaps it helps to imagine the Lord's "terribly frustrating" moments in dealing with us.

Bitter or Better

It is interesting that Moroni shares with us so many of the words of his father, Mormon. Among the statements Mormon made, Moroni himself must have found comfort in his father's counsel:

> For behold, a bitter fountain cannot bring forth good water; neither can a good fountain bring forth bitter water. (Moroni 7:11)

As we've already discussed, Moroni had every reason to feel bitter. His father, family, and "all [his] kinsfolk" were slain in battle (Mormon 8:5). Did Moroni ask, "What have I done to deserve this?" Did he let the unfairness of it all fester until he became bitter at his enemies and even at God? No. In fact, these last ten chapters were written that "they may be of worth unto my brethren, the Lamanites, in some future day" (Moroni 1:4). Did you catch that? Moroni holds no grudge against the Lamanites. He is writing in the hope that the offspring of those who killed his father and kinsfolk will be blessed someday by his words.

Wisdom for dealing with life can be found in strange places. One time, while visiting a touristy gift shop in Juneau, Alaska, I found many gems printed on refrigerator magnets. For example:

> **YOU CAN'T CHANGE THE PAST, BUT YOU CAN DWELL ON IT UNTIL YOU'RE OLD AND ALONE.**

Such a cold statement is perfect for a fridge. (I mean, point taken, but ouch!) As we've already discussed, Moroni came to a point where he deliberately stopped talking about the past and instead looked to the future. Another refrigerator magnet expressed a similar idea, but it was a little more tactful and hopeful:

> **WHILE NO ONE CAN GO BACK AND MAKE A BRAND-NEW BEGINNING, ALL OF US CAN START WHERE WE ARE AND MAKE A BRAND-NEW ENDING.**

Sure, we may be able to convince others that our situation is worse than anyone else's, or that our problems are unfair and unmanageable, or that no one else on earth has any idea what we're going through, but to what end? So that they can excuse our bitterness? And then run away from us because we're too unpleasant to be around? Like Moroni, we must get to a point where we move beyond the past and focus on making a brand-new ending.

As a bishop, more than once I had members express the fear that they had forfeited the promises in their patriarchal blessings because of the mistakes they had made. To me, this is Satan trying to get them to give up and give in to despair and discouragement. The gospel of Jesus Christ is a gospel of new beginnings and second chances. Baptism is being born again. Renewing of covenants at the sacrament table signifies that we're going to get a fresh start in the coming week. I just can't imagine our Heavenly Father saying, "Sorry, you had your chance." If the Lord counseled us to forgive "seventy times seven" (Matthew 18:22), I suspect He is equally forgiving of us. Even if some promised blessings might not be realized in this life, my firm belief is that the Lord can take us wherever we are, help us start again, and allow us to create a brand-new ending with its own promised blessings.

Whether our spiritual wounds are self-inflicted or the result of trials and afflictions beyond our control, our opportunity is to become better rather than bitter. The more we study the lives of prophets ancient and modern, the more we learn how difficult their lives really were. Think about Abraham, Nephi, Abinadi, Joseph Smith, and, of course, Jesus Christ Himself! Their lives were anything but easy. So perhaps we should hope for more difficulties so we can be like them? Uh, no thanks, not this kid. I love what President Heber J. Grant said:

> We sometimes meet people who say they would like to have witnessed the trials of the early Saints and taken a part in them, but I have no wish to nominate myself for a martyr. (In Conference Report, April 1898, 15)

Since a bitter fountain can only bring forth bitter water, any bitterness we feel must be replaced with something better. People and prophets of every age and time have dealt with personal loss, persecution, and problems. Those things are part of the test of earth life. But we revere these stalwarts because they learned to press forward anyway.

Faith, Hope, and Charity

Mormon concluded with some remarks about faith, hope, and charity, a sermon very similar to Paul's epistle in 1 Corinthians 13. Paul taught that "Charity never faileth" (1 Corinthians 13:8), a three-word sermon that has become the motto of the Relief Society.

I love it when scriptures and quotations use strong words like *never, always, first, last,* and *best.*

Imagine how much weaker Paul's phrase would sound if it read, "Charity hardly ever faileth," or "There's a really good chance charity won't fail." Elder Bruce R. McConkie used strong words like *most* and *above all* when he commented on this verse:

> Above all the attributes of godliness and perfection, charity is the one most devoutly to be desired. Charity is more than love, far more; it is everlasting love, perfect love, the pure love of Christ which endureth forever. (*Doctrinal New Testament Commentary*, 3 vols. [1965–73], 2:378)

Since charity *never* fails, we should strive to have it *always*. President Thomas S. Monson used strong words like *everything* and *all* when he taught, "May this long enduring . . . motto, this timeless truth, guide you in everything you do. May it permeate your very souls and find expression in all your thoughts and actions" ("Charity Never Faileth," *Ensign*, November 2010, 125).

In common usage, many think of "faith" as merely an optimism that things will work out. "Hope" is commonly understood as an expectation of a desired outcome, and "charity" is an organization that helps the poor. But faith, hope, and charity have deeper, more specific meanings in a religious context. Elder Jeffrey R. Holland taught:

> What is the nature of this hope? It is certainly much more than wishful thinking. It is to have "hope through the atonement of Christ and the power of his resurrection, to be raised unto life eternal, and this because of your faith in him according to the promise." *That* is the theological meaning of hope in the faith-hope-charity sequence. With an eye to that meaning, Moroni 7:42 then clearly reads, "If a man have faith [in Christ and his atonement] he must needs [as a consequence] have hope [in the promise of the

Resurrection, because the two are inextricably linked]; for without faith [in Christ's atonement] there cannot be any hope [in the Resurrection]." (*Christ and the New Covenant: The Messianic Message of the Book of Mormon* [1997], 334–35.)

Faith is in Christ and His Atonement; *hope* is in the Resurrection, one of the fruits of the Savior's Atonement; and *charity* is the pure love of Christ. The word *of* in the English language is not very precise. For example, is the "pure love of Christ" talking about our love for Him? Our pure love of Christ? Or is the "pure love of Christ" talking about His love for us, as in, "He loves us with the pure love of Christ"? Or, is "the pure love of Christ" a quality of love, as in, "I love my neighbors with the pure love of Christ"? The answer, according to Elder C. Max Caldwell, is "Yes."

I considered what was meant by the phrase "love of Christ." That answer is critical because "the Lord God hath given a commandment that all men should have charity, which charity is love." (2 Ne. 26:30.) If we must have charity, then we must know what it is. The phrase "love of Christ" might have meaning in three dimensions:

1. Love *for* Christ
2. Love *from* Christ
3. Love *like* Christ. ("Love of Christ," *Ensign*, November 1992, 29)

What a wonderful way to approach life! Moroni reminds us to love Christ, to be loved by Him, and to love others as He loves them. A lofty but worthy goal, and a lifetime pursuit. Moroni also showed us the way to judge righteously, such needed advice in a world increasingly looking for new ways to offend and be offended. Moroni not only taught but demonstrated how to conquer bitterness and make a brand-new ending while enveloped in the pure love of Christ.

LIKENING MORONI
Moroni 7

I do not pass *final* judgments on myself or others

I seek to make *intermediate* judgments righteously

I will not let myself become bitter

I seek faith, hope, and charity in Christ

Chapter Eleven

MORONI 8
"Baptism Cometh by Faith"

Moroni chapter 8 is a letter from Mormon that Moroni received "after [his] calling to the ministry" (v.1), so we may suppose that Mormon was Moroni's priesthood leader in some sense. As we all know, this chapter addresses disputations about baptism, and more specifically about the erroneous practice of baptizing children before the age of accountability. For our purposes, we will liken Moroni's inclusion of this chapter as an endorsement and a directive to keep *first things first!*

As painful as it is to say, I have been teaching the Book of Mormon for more than twenty years (which is shocking, since I like to think of myself as perpetually twenty-five years old). One of the things that has impressed me is the prevalence of the first principles of the gospel throughout the text. I suppose I should not be surprised, since the fourth article of faith lists the first principles and ordinances of the gospel plainly, but when my eyes and ears are watching for them in the text, I'm amazed at how often they appear, especially the twin principles "faith and repentance." Perhaps you will be amazed too as you watch for them when you read.

Faith in the Lord Jesus Christ

We remember that the first principle of the gospel is not merely "faith," but "faith in the Lord Jesus Christ." This principle was powerfully impressed upon my family when my oldest brother, David, needed a new kidney. We all believed that perhaps the whole transplant ordeal could be avoided if our faithful and worthy father exercised his priesthood authority and gave my brother a blessing. "Perhaps Dad could simply heal David!" we thought. "We have enough faith!" Later, because my brother was working on an urgent engineering project involving translation technology for the Church, a member of the Quorum of the Seventy was dispatched to pronounce a blessing. "Surely," we thought, "he will heal David because the Church urgently needs these devices my brother has invented!"

Well, the blessing was given, and David was promised some wonderful things, but he wasn't healed. I had the privilege of donating a kidney, and although it wasn't what we had hoped for, wonderful things resulted.

We learned what should have been rather obvious, which is that the first principle of the gospel is not "faith in what we want," or "faith in our own ideas of how things should turn out," but "faith in the Lord Jesus Christ." Faith in the Lord Jesus Christ includes faith in letting His will, His timing, and His methods be done.

In hindsight, we are all delighted with how things unfolded in my family. Promised blessings—miraculous blessings, in fact—were promised and fulfilled, a family grew closer together in wonderful ways, and the Church eventually received the translation technology that sends general conference messages to the world in many languages (see note at the end of this chapter).

If you begin to watch for "faith in Christ" phrases in the scriptures, you will begin to notice them everywhere! Four quick examples:

- When Enos's sins were forgiven, his first question was, "Lord, how is it done?" The answer, "because of thy faith in Christ" (Enos 1:7–8).
- When Captain Moroni called a cease-fire and confronted Zerahemnah, he explained the Nephites' military and strategic success by stating, "And now I would that ye should understand that this is done unto us because of our religion and our faith in Christ" (Alma 44:3; notice how many times Moroni references faith in verses 3–4).
- When Alma and Amulek approached Zeezrom, their one-time adversary turned believer, who was "very low with a burning fever," they healed him while crying, "O Lord our God, have mercy on this man, and heal him according to his faith which is in Christ" (Alma 15:5, 10).
- Alma taught his son Helaman what to teach the people: "Teach them to withstand every temptation of the devil, with their faith on the Lord Jesus Christ" (Alma 37:33).

More examples could be given, but the point is clear. It doesn't really matter what challenges or what righteous desires you have, the first step is always faith in the Lord Jesus Christ. As Elder John H. Groberg taught, "When we exercise faith in the Lord Jesus Christ, we can do things we could not otherwise do" ("The Lord's Wind," *Ensign*, November 1993, 28). Someone with great faith once pointed out the difference between wanting what we want and wanting what God wants when they said, "You can either have what you want, or you can have something better."

First Principles Deserve First Attention

Our challenge is living in the latter days with an overwhelming number of tasks to do, roles to fulfill, and priorities to juggle. If we are not careful, many second-class things get first-class attention. If the Book of Mormon gives such first-class attention to first principles, we should do likewise. For example, in some circles, I see the temptation to give more attention to Book of Mormon geography than to Book of Mormon theology. Personally, I love the geology, the archeology, the word studies, the parallelisms, the word-print studies, the chiasmus structures, the Hebraisms, and all the other "-isms" involved in studying the text of the Book of Mormon. Seriously, I eat this stuff up! It strengthens my testimony. But if I go home and act like an impatient, irritable tyrant to my spouse and children, then I have clearly missed the central message of the Book of Mormon, and I need to give more first-class attention to first-class things. And what are those first-class things? First principles and ordinances: first, faith in Jesus Christ; second, repentance; third, baptism; and fourth, the gift of the Holy Ghost. (The first principles and ordinances of the gospel are not faith, repentance, baptism, and the location of Zarahemla.)

Faith in Christ is the first principle—an ongoing effort and an ongoing blessing. Perhaps that's why we call it "exercising" faith. Elder Vaughn J. Featherstone taught:

> Number one on our agenda, above all else, is faith in Christ. I don't know anything that will take the place of it. Whenever we find problems in the Church, we usually find them under one of two umbrellas or canopies, either transgression or lack of faith in Christ. ("The Torchbearer," *BYU Devotional Speeches of the Year* [1982–83], 145)

Following faith in Christ is repentance. The word *repent*, Elder Jeffrey R. Holland said, is "perhaps the most hopeful and encouraging word in the Christian vocabulary" ("Broken Things to Mend," *Ensign*, May 2006, 70). To repent is to turn or to change direction. Repentance is also an ongoing effort and blessing, and more a way of life than an event. Faith in Christ leads to repentance because our Savior's Atonement makes repentance possible. Pondering the Savior's love for us leads to humility and a desire to change for the better. Elder David B. Haight taught:

> If we could feel or were sensitive in the slightest to the matchless love of our Savior and his willingness to suffer for our individual sins, we would cease procrastination and "clean the slate," and repent of all our transgressions. ("Our Lord and Savior," *Ensign*, May 1988, 23)

The Event of Baptism and the Process of Being Born Again

Repentance must become a way of life. Baptism, on the other hand, is not thought of as a way of life, but more as a one-time event, because it is. However, if we remember that we have the opportunity to renew our baptismal covenants every Sabbath day, then we begin to think of our baptism as a symbol of an ongoing commitment. Our baptismal covenants include our promise to mourn with those that mourn, to comfort those who stand in need of comfort, and to stand as witnesses of God at all times, in all things, and in all places (see Mosiah 18:9). So while our baptism date may be long past, our baptismal covenants continue and are also ongoing efforts. We often think of being born again and baptism as synonymous, but they are not. Alma asked the saints in Zarahemla, "My brethren *of the church*, have ye spiritually been born of God?" (Alma 5:14; emphasis added). If they were members of the Church, they had obviously been baptized, but Alma wondered if they had been born again. Baptism is an important life event, but being "born again" is the process of being converted, a lifelong process that begins at baptism.

Finally, of course, is the second part of our baptism, the "baptism of fire," or the laying on of hands for the gift of the Holy Ghost. The Lord's promise of divine companionship is repeated by the priests at the sacrament table each Sunday when they pronounce that we may "always have his Spirit to be with [us]" (Moroni 4:3).

Our ongoing effort to keep the Spirit with us concludes our list of first things first as expressed in the fourth article of faith. When our heads are spinning with all we have to do, when our various roles are competing for our time and attention, how nice to have these divine priorities spelled out for us! If we ever wonder exactly what our priorities are, or what they should be, it is helpful to remember that our priorities are directly connected to our covenants. Interestingly, many centuries ago, the ancient Saints subscribed to the same divine priorities. Another insight to help us survive turbulent times!

LIKENING MORONI
Moroni 8

I will nurture my faith in Christ

I will make repentance a way of life

I will remember my baptismal covenants

I will rejoice in the blessing of the Holy Ghost

I will strive to give first-class
attention to first-class things

Note: If you'd like to see the translation device my brother David invented, go to lds.org and enter a search for the video "Special Witness—Elder Ballard." Or, enter this URL: https://www.lds.org/media-library/video/2011-04-20 -special-witness-elder-ballard?lang=eng. At the 1:37 mark, you will see an electronic component labeled with the logo "dlb research." The DLB stands for David L. Bytheway.

Chapter Twelve

MORONI 9
"Notwithstanding Their Hardness, Let Us Labor Diligently"

Moroni shares with us Mormon's second epistle, a tender father-to-son letter, in Moroni chapter 9. In this letter, Mormon speaks of the moral decline of his people and of their recent defeats on the field of battle. Through it all, Mormon has not stopped trying to preach the word of God, but he expresses his frustration regarding the reaction of those to whom he has spoken:

> When I speak the word of God with sharpness they tremble and anger against me; and when I use no sharpness they harden their hearts against it. (Moroni 9:4)

Mormon finds that no matter how he attempts to preach the gospel, with tenderness or boldness, it falls on closed ears and hardened hearts. This situation is not new or surprising. We are reminded of the Apostle Peter on the day of Pentecost, and the different reactions he received while sharing his witness of Christ:

- Some were "amazed"
- Some were "in doubt" (or "perplexed," New International Version)
- Some were "mocking"
- Some "gladly received his word" and were baptized (Acts 2:12–13, 41)

These scriptural accounts help us prepare future missionaries for the different reactions they may receive as they share the happy message of the Restoration. All of us wish we could be more eloquent, more brilliant, more polished in presenting the gospel. Ofttimes, after we try to share the gospel or a spiritual thought with a stranger or coworker, we replay the encounter in our minds over and over again, wishing we had said things differently, perhaps with more boldness, more kindness, or a better choice of words. We may find some comfort when we remember that even Jesus, the master teacher, did not convert everyone He spoke to. Joseph F. Smith observed:

The Savior spent about three years in his ministry among the Jews and those of the house of Israel, endeavoring to teach them the everlasting gospel and call them unto repentance; and yet, notwithstanding his mighty works, and miracles, and proclamation of the truth, in great power and authority, there were but few who hearkened to his voice, and rejoiced in his presence, and received salvation at his hands. (D&C 138:25–26)

Mormon's situation, his people in moral and spiritual decline, his efforts to minister being rejected, all lead to this marvelous seven-word statement: "Notwithstanding their hardness, let us labor diligently" (Moroni 9:6). These seven words are worth reading again, slowly, emphasizing the pronouns *their* and *us*.

Our behavior is just that—ours. We cannot allow our reactions to be dictated by others' actions. As Stephen Covey taught, "Between stimulus and response, there is a space. And in that space lies our freedom to choose our response" (*The 8th Habit* [2004], 42). We are not animals subject to the "stimulus/response" model. We have agency. And even if we feel we have every *right* to act the way we do, we also have the option not to. We choose our responses to all of life's stimuli. We can either act or be acted upon (see 2 Nephi 2:13). So, to paraphrase Mormon, "Notwithstanding everything they're doing out there, let us choose to behave according to true principles."

Another refrigerator magnet I saw contained this gem:

> **NEVER PUT THE KEY**
> **TO YOUR HAPPINESS IN**
> **SOMEONE ELSE'S POCKET.**

Easier said than done? Yes. Deliberately or not, we often put others in charge of our happiness. Or we allow situations or circumstances to dictate our mood. I suspect we all, myself included, permit this to happen from time to time. One of the craziest examples of our being affected by the behavior of others is in the world of sports. Can the behavior and actions of eleven guys you don't know, and whom you have never met, make or ruin your whole weekend? Yes, if they are a football team—or *your* football team, as the marketing department would have you call them. Because when "your" team wins, then somehow you are a winner too; and if you "buy" into this sort of vicarious heroism, you might also "buy" more merchandise. Perhaps that's why sports enthusiasts are called "fans" (a shortened form of "fanatics").

"He makes me mad," or "She makes me crazy," or "They make me want to scream" are all different ways of saying the same thing: You have placed the key to your happiness in someone else's pocket. They cannot really "make" you anything. Mormon advises, "Notwithstanding *their* behavior, let *us* choose to behave better."

I used to listen to a popular radio show about families and relationships, and I noticed that the host often received the same type of questions from callers: "My in-laws are like this, and I have a hard time with how they act, and at Thanksgiving, should I do this or should I do this . . . ?" They were usually interrupted by the host, who would always answer with something similar to Mormon's advice: "You be sweet and nice and polite and help clean up, and you don't have to go again until next year." In other words, it's not about *their* behavior! You can't change that. It's about *yours!* Perhaps their behavior is reprehensible and unfair and wrong. So what? Should it dictate your behavior? Or should your behavior be governed by true principles? Should you do what you feel like doing, or should you do what's right?

It is interesting that Moroni heard this message not only from his earthly father but from the Savior as well. Moroni was worried about how others, "they," might respond to imperfections in the record. The Lord answered:

> If *they* have not charity it mattereth not unto *thee, thou* hast been faithful. (Ether 12:37; emphasis added)

You cannot control or predict *their* behavior, so don't *you* worry about it. *You* do what is right regardless of what *they* do.

We can liken Moroni's action to ourselves by not worrying so much about *them* and *they*, but about ourselves. We can "do what is right; let the consequence follow" (*Hymns* [1985], no. 237) rather than doing what is popular or what is designed to appease the crowds or get clicks and "likes." To paraphrase Joshua, regardless of what *they* do, as for *us* and *our* house, *we* will choose the Lord (see Joshua 24:15).

Go Down Swinging

As we look at Mormon and Moroni's situation, we may ask, "Why?" Why did they keep working when it all seemed so fruitless? Their own people were ignoring them and probably disliked them. Why did Mormon continue to preach, and why did he advise Moroni to do the same? Mormon answers: "For we have a labor to perform whilst in this tabernacle of clay" (Moroni 9:6). In other words, we will be responsible for our actions, notwithstanding theirs! The baseball expression is to "go down swinging," and the spiritual version might be to "endure to the end."

I remember hearing a Jewish legend about a missionary in Sodom and Gomorrah. He preached and preached with no success, as you might imagine (it was a hard area). Finally, someone asked him, "Why do you continue to try to convert these people? No one is listening to you." "At first," the missionary answered, "I preached so that I might convert one of them. Now, I continue to preach so that they won't convert me." So he continued to labor. It was vital that he continue to labor!

Because agency is involved in every human interaction, it is unwise to measure our success based on the reactions of others. Additionally, it is unwise to set personal goals that rely on the actions of others. Elder Dallin H. Oaks, speaking at the Missionary Training Center in Provo, Utah, gave some wonderful counsel that I wish I had heard when I wore the black name tag:

> We are often asked, "What is a successful missionary?" I want to tell you, there are measures of success of missionaries and of missions, which are very popular and very misplaced. I want to tell you what the successful measure of a missionary is. It is the best you can do each day, regardless of the outcome.
>
> Missionary success should never be measured by the exercise of someone else's agency. If you present yourself according to mission rules and procedures and according to the instructions of your leaders, and do the best you can to teach, it does not matter whether anyone you teach ever is baptized into the Church. It does not matter to your success. It matters, of course, to them and to other things. But if you are trying to measure your success as a missionary, do not measure it by the exercise of someone else's agency. If you do,

you will be tempted to infringe upon that agency in one way or another, and that is not appropriate. (MTC Devotional, September 21, 1999)

In other words, set mission goals (and life goals) that focus on your behavior, not the behavior of others. Set personal goals based on things you can do, not on what others might or might not do. Notwithstanding *their* reactions, *you* continue to labor faithfully.

Don't Let It Get You Down

It would be hard to characterize Mormon's report in this chapter regarding the decaying situation of the Nephites as anything but a "downer." The horrifying depravity and descriptions of cannibalism, torture, and rape would grieve anyone with a heart. At the close of his heartbreaking epistle, we sense the love between these two souls, sharing family bonds but also ecclesiastical responsibilities, both having been called to the ministry. It is impossible to say for sure, but this could have been one of Mormon's last letters to his son, and he chooses to conclude on a higher note:

My son, be faithful in Christ; and may not the things which I have written grieve thee, to weigh thee down unto death; but may Christ lift thee up, and may his sufferings and death, and the showing his body unto our fathers, and his mercy and long-suffering, and the hope of his glory and of eternal life, rest in your mind forever. (Moroni 9:25)

What a beautiful thought! When the world gets you down, let Christ lift you up. And what's more, let His mission and victory over death and sin "rest in your mind forever." What else could possibly rest in our minds that would bring greater comfort than the testimony of Christ? With all we are witnessing in the latter days, I have always loved the statement of President Boyd K. Packer:

This is a great time to live. When times are unsettled, when the dangers persist, the Lord pours out His blessings upon His Church and kingdom. . . . I have been associated now in the councils of the Church for nearly twenty years. During that time I have seen, from the sidelines at least, many a crisis. I have seen, at times, great disappointment, some concern, maybe at times some anxiety. One thing I have never seen is fear. Fear is the antithesis of faith. In this Church and in this kingdom, there is faith. ("Ordinances," *BYU Speeches* [1980], 17)

All of the counsel we have received over the years regarding daily prayer and daily scripture study is perhaps to allow the Savior and His gospel to "rest in our minds"— and to be comfortable there. Interestingly, the scriptures teach us to think our thoughts according to a plan, not to let them be random or tossed about. For example, "Look unto me in every thought; doubt not, fear not," concludes a revelation to Oliver Cowdery (D&C 6:36), and, of course, there's Paul's admonition:

> Finally, brethren, whatsoever things are true, whatsoever things are honest, whatsoever things are just, whatsoever things are pure, whatsoever things are lovely, whatsoever things are of good report; if there be any virtue, and if there be any praise, *think on these things*. (Philippians 4:8; emphasis added)

The thirteenth article of faith, which mentions Paul's admonition, concludes, "We seek after these things." Paul's advice reminds us to "think on these things," or to think our thoughts according to a plan.

If we do so, and allow the peace and joy and power of the gospel to rest in our minds, we should not be surprised when we feel more peaceful, more joyful, and more powerful.

What gems from Moroni! I will not be held accountable for the world's behavior, but I will be for my own. I can control only my own behavior, so I will exercise my own faith and look to Christ to lift me up.

LIKENING MORONI
Moroni 9

Notwithstanding *their* behavior, *I* will act in faith

I do not focus on what I cannot control

I will not let events get me down;
I will let Christ lift me up

Chapter Thirteen

MORONI 10
"Every Good Gift Cometh of Christ"

Moroni's final chapter contains Moroni's promise, an explanation of spiritual gifts, a final invitation, and a stirring farewell.

Ask average members of the Church to tell you something they know about Moroni chapter 10, and they will probably respond, "Moroni's promise." It is hard to estimate the impact of Moroni's promise on missionary work. We might say that Moroni 10:3–4 is as important to gaining a testimony of the Book of Mormon as James 1:5 was to bringing about the Restoration. President Gordon B. Hinckley observed:

> No other book contains such a promise. If Moroni had written nothing else, this promise in his concluding testimony would mark him

forever as an eloquent witness of eternal truth.
For, said he, "by the power of the Holy Ghost ye
may know the truth of all things" (Moroni 10:5).
(*Teachings of Presidents of the Church: Gordon B.
Hinckley* [2016], 227)

Before offering his formula for inviting the Holy
Ghost to confirm the truth of the record, Moroni invites us to "remember how merciful the Lord hath
been unto the children of men, from the creation of
Adam even down until the time that ye shall receive
these things" (Moroni 10:3).

From the creation of Adam until now? That's a siz-
able chunk of time. In other words, remind yourself of
God's mercy since Adam, the first man. Since the Book
of Mormon gives only minimal information about
Adam, Noah, Moses, and so forth, it would seem that
Moroni is asking us to ponder God's dealings with man
from all available sources—which for us would mean
the Bible, the Pearl of Great Price, and the Doctrine
and Covenants as well. What are the scriptures? How
would we describe them? How about a record of the
Lord's mercy to His children?

We sing the words, "Count your blessings, name
them one by one, and it will surprise you what the

Lord has done" (Hymns [1985], no. 241). Perhaps a similar result can be obtained by "counting your tender mercies," naming them one by one. God has indeed been merciful to us by "preserving [us] from day to day, by lending [us] breath" (Mosiah 2:21). But the pinnacle of all His mercies was what an angel called the "condescension of God" (1 Nephi 11:16, 26). Nephi beheld that the very Son of God would suffer Himself to be judged by a wicked world, mocked, scourged, and crucified. Why would he do that? Nephi, having witnessed the awful events in a vision, gave the "why" a few chapters later:

> And the world, because of their iniquity, shall judge him to be a thing of naught; wherefore they scourge him, and he suffereth it; and they smite him, and he suffereth it. Yea, they spit upon him, and he suffereth it, because of his loving kindness and his long-suffering towards the children of men. (1 Nephi 19:9)

Notice, it wasn't a sense of duty or obligation that helped the Lord endure such unspeakable suffering, but His love and His patience with us. He preferred to suffer Himself rather than to see us suffer, "For behold, I, God, have suffered these things for all, that they might not suffer if they would repent" (D&C 19:16). We have been the recipients of the Savior's loving kindness and longsuffering, but, so generously, He offers more.

Spiritual Gifts

Next, Moroni speaks of spiritual gifts available to Heavenly Father's children. Have you ever discovered an unopened gift under the Christmas tree a few days *after* Christmas? Have you experienced the joy and anticipation of Christmas morning all over again as you opened it? The Lord has showered us not only with mercies but also with gifts—gifts that we may not have recognized or acknowledged unless they were pointed out.

The gifts of which Moroni speaks are not Crock-Pots and neckties, but the "best gifts," which we are admonished to "seek earnestly" (D&C 46:8). However, like unnoticed presents on Christmas morning, they may go unseen and unsought because we forget they are there.

Moroni mentions gifts of teaching, faith, healing, prophesying, tongues, and more (see Moroni 10:9–16; a similar list can be found in D&C 46:11–25). Some of our gifts are discovered over time, some are cultivated, some are mentioned in our patriarchal blessings. Sadly, some are neglected because our earthly "to-do" list can overwhelm our days and occupy our time. Moroni reminds us to seek these gifts and declares that "every good gift cometh of Christ" (Moroni 10:18).

Moroni 10 is always a reminder to seek spiritual gifts, a reminder that many of us need. It is as if the Lord is saying, "These gifts are here, these gifts are available; are you seeking them earnestly? Have you forgotten about them?" or, in my words, "Have you left them under the tree, unopened?"

See You There

I don't know exactly how the following meetings will take place, but I'm looking forward to them already. The four major writers of the Book of Mormon are Nephi, Jacob, Mormon, and Moroni. Three of the four mention specifically that they will meet us one day.

Nephi: Christ will show unto you, with power and great glory, that they are his words, at the last day; and you and I shall stand face to face before his bar; and ye shall know that I have been commanded of him to write these things, notwithstanding my weakness. (2 Nephi 33:11)

Jacob: Finally, I bid you farewell, until I shall meet you before the pleasing bar of God, which bar striketh the wicked with awful dread and fear. Amen. (Jacob 6:13)

Moroni says he will meet us as well. How exciting! But he won't be doing the talking:

Moroni: The Lord God will say unto you: Did I not declare my words unto you, which were written by this man, like as one crying from the dead, yea, even as one speaking out of the dust? (Moroni 10:27)

Clearly, these words are addressed to those who have had the opportunity to read the Book of Mormon, as we have. The Lord refers to Moroni as "this man." Will we know the identity of "this man" when the Lord points him out? I love this story told by Elder Russell M. Nelson, who, after touring the Ogden Temple Open House, wanted to know if his children knew who Moroni was:

In the evening, at the end of our tour of the Ogden Temple, our family enjoyed a view as we departed. I asked the children: What is that golden figure standing atop the spire of the temple? Who does that represent? Almost in unison, they replied, "The angel Moroni!" I was pleased. They knew his name. (*Accomplishing the Impossible* [2015], 18)

Hopefully, we will be acquainted with Moroni's work and Moroni's promise to the point that we may be able to answer the Lord that indeed Moroni's words have been declared unto us, and that we loved them, pondered them, respected them, and shared them.

Awake and Arise

Dozens of verses of scripture begin with the word *awake*, and, oddly enough, they are written to people who are already awake—physically, that is. Obviously, the scriptural command to awake is directed at our spirits. It's too easy to be going through the motions physically while spiritually sleepwalking.

Moroni directs the daughters of Zion to "put on [their] beautiful garments," to "strengthen [their] stakes" and "enlarge [their] borders" (Moroni 10:31). (It is important to note here that symbolically all of us, both brothers and sisters, are called "the daughters of

Zion," since Christ is the bridegroom and the Church is the bride.)

A quick glance at the footnotes reveals that Moroni is using language from two different Isaiah chapters (52 and 54), but interestingly, he's putting these phrases side by side in one verse for us. Why would he do that? Let's convert Isaiah's King-James English to modern-day English, and perhaps we will see more clearly what Moroni is telling us to do:

PUT ON THY BEAUTIFUL GARMENTS—
REDEEM THE DEAD

STRENGTHEN THY STAKES—
PERFECT THE SAINTS

ENLARGE THY BORDERS—
PROCLAIM THE GOSPEL

One of Moroni's final appeals is for latter-day readers to "awake" and engage in the mission of the Church. (It is important to note that in recent years, the leaders of the Church have added to the mission of the Church the Savior's admonition to "Care for the Poor and Needy," which is also a theme of the Book of

Mormon.) Having earlier endorsed the Church as an organization, and even described some of its practices, Moroni here encourages future readers to remain engaged and involved in the Church's mission.

The Divine Invitation

Finally, Moroni extends the invitation of all invitations: "Come unto Christ, and be perfected in him" (Moroni 10:32).

A few years ago, while doing some research for a youth talk, I performed a computer search for every occurrence of the phrase *Come unto Christ* and the more personal version of it, *Come unto me*, where Jesus Christ is speaking or being quoted. I learned some wonderful things. First of all, I found twenty-eight total examples of those phrases in the standard works. Guess how many of those twenty-eight were in the Book of Mormon? Twenty-five (or about 89 percent). As Elder David A. Bednar observed:

> The central and recurring theme of the Book of Mormon is the invitation for all to "come unto Christ, and be perfected in him." ("A Reservoir of Living Water," Church Educational System Fireside, February 4, 2007)

Learning how frequently the phrase *come unto me* occurred was interesting, but when I began to notice how different and how wonderful the reasons or rewards for coming unto Christ were, I was stunned. The variety of promises for accepting Christ's invitation were all over the board. Everything you could possibly hope for on your spiritual wish list was there. Observe just a few:

"Come unto me," and:

- "I will give you rest" (Matthew 11:28)
- "drink [living water]" (John 7:37)
- "buy milk and honey, without money" (2 Nephi 26:25)
- "I [will] make weak things become strong" (Ether 12:27)
- "I shall heal [you]" (3 Nephi 18:32)
- "partake of the goodness of God" (Jacob 1:7)
- "I will be merciful unto [you]" (2 Nephi 28:32)
- "stand spotless" (3 Nephi 27:20)
- "know of the true points of my doctrine" (3 Nephi 21:6)
- "ye shall be spared" (Mormon 3:2)
- "have everlasting life" (D&C 45:5)

- "there is a place prepared for you in the mansions of my Father" (Enos 1:27)
- "I will show unto you the greater things" (Ether 4:13)
- "see my face and know that I am" (D&C 93:1)

What more could anyone possibly desire? The best things we could ever want all come after the invitation, "Come unto Christ." Looking at this list, we are reminded of the words of Mormon, who said that "in Christ there should come *every* good thing" (Moroni 7:22; emphasis added). By contrast, Amulek declared, "[the devil] rewardeth you *no* good thing" (Alma 34:39; emphasis added). Thus, the decision of coming unto Christ becomes perhaps the ultimate no-brainer.

Notice the words that follow Moroni's invitation: "Come unto Christ, and be perfected in him." Note the sequence—it is not "be perfected on your own, then come," but "come . . . and be perfected *in him*." Some may think, "Well, I just can't come to Christ right now. I'm too messed up. I've got to get my act together; then I'll come." But this invitation says, "Come as you are, wherever you are, just as you are," and let the perfecting process begin later. As Elder Jeffrey R. Holland observed:

Please realize that the Church is not a monastery for perfect people, though all of us ought to be striving on the road to godliness. No, at least one aspect of the Church is more like a hospital or an aid station, provided for those who are ill and want to get well, where one can get an infusion of spiritual nutrition and a supply of sustaining water in order to keep on climbing. ("He Hath Filled the Hungry with Good Things," *Ensign*, November 1997, 66)

Moroni further invites, "Deny yourselves of all ungodliness" (Moroni 10:32). Perhaps the most important word in this phrase is *yourselves*. Recently, I had a conversation with a mother who was worried about her teenage son. "He just doesn't like being told what to do," she said, and "he perceives the Church as always telling him what to do." But notice, Moroni does not say, "The *For the Strength of Youth* Police will deny you of all ungodliness," or "Your leaders will be watching you and denying you of all ungodliness," but you will deny *yourself!*

We remember when Joseph Smith was asked how

he governed the Saints, he gave this historic answer: "I teach them correct principles and they govern *themselves*." One of the unspoken lessons of Lehi's dream is that the entire metaphor is a grand illustration of agency. No one is herding people to the tree of life, and no one is forcing anyone into the great and spacious building. The dream is full of choices—the tree, the building, strange roads, forbidden paths—and you get to take your pick. The world loves the word *choice* in these latter days, too often confusing liberty with license. Why are the wicked bothered by the choices of the righteous if they are so into choice?

Interestingly, the mocking voices deriding the choices of others are not coming from the tree of life, but from the great and spacious building. Lehi beckoned, but he never mocked. Choice and agency are part of the plan of salvation, but choice is coupled with consequences, which is why Elder Neal A. Maxwell once observed, "We'd better want the consequences of what we want" ("'Swallowed Up in the Will of the Father,'" *Ensign*, November 1995, 23).

"If ye will deny yourselves of all ungodliness," Moroni, assures, "then is his grace sufficient for you." We are unquestionably saved by the grace of Christ.

When it comes to salvation, we are "all beggars," as King Benjamin taught (Mosiah 4:19). The good works we do are part of our theology, but we can never earn our way to heaven through works alone. We might say it this way: first we come *to* Christ, just as we are, then we strive to become *like* Christ. Why? Because He asked us to! "What manner of men ought ye to be? Verily I say unto you, even as I am" (3 Nephi 27:27). The coming to Christ has already been done. We have entered the gate and are on the path. Now the lifelong process of striving to become *like* Christ begins, and it is impossible to become like Christ without Christ's help.

Moroni begins the very last verse of the entire Book of Mormon with this farewell: "I soon go to rest in the paradise of God" (Moroni 10:34). A well-deserved rest, we might add. Moroni buried the plates in AD 421, more than three decades after the final battle at Cumorah. Not only had he been wandering "for the safety of [his] own life" (Moroni 1:3) for all those years, but he had also had to safeguard the sacred records as well. It must have felt wonderful to etch "I soon go to rest" upon the plates. Interestingly, Moroni's work concerning this record would continue after his mortal death.

LIKENING MORONI
Moroni 10

I seek truth through the Holy Ghost

I seek earnestly the best gifts

I participate in the mission of the Church

I will come unto Christ and be perfected in Him

Chapter Fourteen

Immortal Moroni

As we all know, Moroni's story did not conclude after he buried the plates. He returned under the direction of the Lord in the latter days on numerous occasions to tutor young Joseph Smith and eventually to deliver the record. Now a resurrected being, Moroni's return to earth was glorious:

> He had on a loose robe of most exquisite whiteness. It was a whiteness beyond anything earthly I had ever seen; nor do I believe that any earthly thing could be made to appear so exceedingly white and brilliant. His hands were naked, and his arms also, a little above the wrist; so, also, were his feet naked, as were his legs, a little above the ankles. His head and neck were also bare. I could

discover that he had no other clothing on but this robe, as it was open, so that I could see into his bosom. Not only was his robe exceedingly white, but his whole person was glorious beyond description, and his countenance truly like lightning. The room was exceedingly light, but not so very bright as immediately around his person. When I first looked upon him, I was afraid; but the fear soon left me. (Joseph Smith—History 1:31–32)

While Moroni may not have known until the unexpected death of his father the prominent role he would play in the latter-day Restoration, no doubt the Lord knew all along. The Savior speaks of His own return to earth in these words:

Marvel not, for the hour cometh that I will drink of the fruit of the vine with you on the earth, and with Moroni, whom I have sent unto you to reveal the Book of Mormon, containing the fulness of my everlasting gospel, to whom I have committed the keys of the record of the stick of Ephraim. (D&C 27:5)

Interestingly, although it was Mormon who did most of the abridging, the keys of the "stick of

Ephraim," to use Ezekiel's phrase, were conferred upon Moroni (see Ezekiel 37:16). It was Moroni who was sent to tell young Joseph that God had a work for him to do, it was Moroni who visited and taught Joseph over a four-year period, and it was Moroni who took the record when the translation was finished.

How might we summarize Moroni's message? To me, it is this— stay the course. Come to Christ, receive the Holy Ghost, receive the priesthood ordinances, and be where you are supposed to be. Stand in holy places and hold onto eternal truth even when it may be more fashionable to question everything and reject anything that is old and established, doesn't have a hashtag, or has been around for more than twenty years. Whether your problems are minor or major, whether you are single or married, young or old, the answers are the same. Take advantage of what Pahoran called the "great privilege of our church" (Alma 61:14), wherein the blessings of the priesthood, the ordinances, and the warm fellowship reside.

A brief but powerful "stay the course" message was given by Elder Glenn L. Pace, a modern Church leader whose words I have found to be increasingly applicable as time goes on. Elder Pace spoke of the Church as a train:

> It is as if we are passengers on the train of the Church, which has been moving forward gradually and methodically. Sometimes we have looked out the window and thought, "That looks kind of fun out there. This train is so restrictive." So we have jumped off and gone and played in the woods for a while. Sooner or later we find it isn't as much fun as Lucifer makes it appear or we get critically injured, so we work our way back to the tracks and see the train ahead. With a determined sprint we catch up to it, breathlessly wipe the perspiration from our forehead, and thank the Lord for repentance.

> While on the train we can see the world and some of our own members outside laughing and having a great time. They taunt us and coax us to get off. Some throw logs and rocks on the tracks to try and derail it. Other members run alongside the tracks, and while they may never go play in the woods, they just can't seem to get on the train. Others try to run ahead and too often take the wrong turn.

I would propose that the luxury of getting on and off the train as we please is fading. The speed of the train is increasing. The woods are getting much too dangerous, and the fog and darkness are moving in. ("Spiritual Revival," *Ensign*, November 1992, 11–12)

Elder Pace's plea is the same as Moroni's. Stay on the train! Too many are running alongside, running ahead, and even running away. The danger is, if we don't make up our minds and get on board, the Church will be running away from us. And yes, the woods are getting dark and dangerous, and the fog and darkness are moving in. If you have been away from the Church for a while, I hope you'll come back. Get on board. We don't have any perfect passengers, but we will offer you what we have. Yes, you need the Church, but the Church also needs you. Other members need you. Fellowship is not just a nice side effect of Church membership, it is part of it. We cannot mourn with those who mourn and comfort those who stand in need of comfort if we do not know who they are.

I still watch for Moroni as I drive down the freeway. Living in Utah, I see him frequently. I experience an even greater thrill when I have the chance to travel outside of Utah and see one of our temples gleaming in the night. And there he is again, Moroni, with a trumpet in one hand and the plates in the other, seemingly floating above the trees, like "another angel fly[ing] in the midst of heaven," as John prophesied (Revelation 14:6). Sister Elaine Dalton, who served as Young Women General President and had an office near the temple, taught:

> Every day I see the angel Moroni standing atop the temple as a shining symbol of not only his faith but ours. I love Moroni because, in a very degenerate society, he remained pure and true. He is my hero. He stood alone. I feel somehow he stands atop the temple today, beckoning us to have courage, to remember who we are, and to be worthy to enter the holy temple—to "arise and shine forth," to stand above the worldly clamor, and to, as Isaiah prophesied, "Come . . . to the mountain of the Lord"—the holy temple. ("Now Is the Time to Arise and Shine," *Ensign*, May 2012, 123)

"I did liken all scriptures unto us," Nephi explained, "that it might be for our profit and learning" (1 Nephi 19:23). The word *liken* is not used very often outside of the scriptures. I suppose there are as many ways to "liken" the scriptures as there are "likeners," and this book is no exception. Likening can be a wonderfully personal experience. Not everyone will liken scriptural stories in the same way, nor should they. This book was simply my effort to find personal meaning in Moroni's message. In sharing these ideas, I am hoping others may find them helpful and have something to think about as they ponder their own ways to liken Moroni's final words.

Next time you pass by a temple, I hope you will lift up your eyes and see Moroni, our brother in the gospel. In that moment, my hope is that your heart will swell with love and admiration for this valiant witness of Jesus Christ who did so much to proclaim the gospel while by himself but never really alone.

Likening Moroni

What is Moroni's message? Have you been through something difficult? Has your faith taken a hit? Have you been thrown against the wall by life? We all have turbulent times personally, and we live in turbulent times in the world today. To survive these times, try *likening Moroni:*

MORMON 8	I will stop rehearsing my past
	I will remember my identity
	I will find my mission
	I will look forward to the future
	I will humbly accept the will of the Lord
	I will cleanse the inner vessel

MORMON 9	I will believe in Christ I will live after the manner of happiness I will learn wisdom from the experience of others
ETHER 1–15	I will maintain my faith in Christ I will not try to conquer my weakness alone—I will confess my weakness before the Lord, and He will make weak things strong
MORONI 1	I do not enter enemy territory I will not deny the Christ I give something of worth to the future
MORONI 2	I will receive the Holy Ghost I will recognize that I am never really alone I will trust the Holy Ghost as my warning light, my tutor, my weapon, and my protector
MORONI 3	I acknowledge the blessings of the priesthood in my midst I value the priesthood and the ordinances and blessings it makes available

MORONI 4-5	I will renew my covenants often by partaking of the sacrament I will remember the Savior's sacrifice I strive to be worthy of the promise of His companionship I look forward with hope to the restoration and resurrection made possible by the Savior
MORONI 6	I embrace organized religion I am active in both the Church and the gospel I am numbered and remembered, and I remember others by home and visiting teaching I meet often with fellow Saints to remember the Savior and to discuss the welfare of my soul I am nourished by the good word
MORONI 7	I do not pass *final* judgments on myself or others I seek to make *intermediate* judgments righteously I will not let myself become bitter I seek faith, hope, and charity in Christ

MORONI 8	I will nurture my faith in Christ I will make repentance a way of life I will remember my baptismal covenants I will rejoice in the blessing of the Holy Ghost I will strive to give first-class attention to first-class things
MORONI 9	Notwithstanding *their* behavior, *I* will act in faith I do not focus on what I cannot control I will not let events get me down; I will let Christ lift me up
MORONI 10	I seek truth through the Holy Ghost I seek earnestly the best gifts I participate in the mission of the Church I will come unto Christ and be perfected in Him

About the Author

JOHN BYTHEWAY served a mission to the Philippines and later graduated from Brigham Young University. He has a master's degree in religious education and is a part-time instructor at the BYU Salt Lake Center. John is the author of many best-selling books, audio talks, and DVDs, including *Of Pigs, Pearls, and Prodigals: A Fresh Look at the Parables of Jesus; Finding Your Path in Lehi's Dream; Isaiah for Airheads;* and *Righteous Warriors: Lessons from the War Chapters in the Book of Mormon.* He and his wife, Kimberly, have six children.